Poems 1927–1929

W. H. AUDEN

Poems

1927–1929

A PHOTOGRAPHIC AND TYPOGRAPHIC FACSIMILE
OF THE ORIGINAL NOTEBOOK IN THE
BERG COLLECTION
OF ENGLISH AND AMERICAN LITERATURE

Edited by

PATRICK T. LAWLOR

With an Introduction by

NICHOLAS JENKINS

The New York Public Library

1989

International Standard Book Number 0–87104–415–3

The Harcourt Brace Jovanovich Fund

for Publications Based on Manuscripts
in the Berg Collection
of English and American Literature
in The New York Public Library

Publication Number Three

Contents

Foreword

To us he is no more a person / now but a whole climate of opinion.[1]

THESE LINES by W. H. Auden about Sigmund Freud might well, by now, apply to him. But in looking back at his poetic beginnings, we may take the word of an exiled Russian poet, Joseph Brodsky, and think of Auden as "the greatest mind of the twentieth century." His poetry, spanning some forty-five years, reflects not only the universally human, but also all the complexities and horrors of the twentieth century. In prose, and on the stage, the poet's individual voice always resounded, and it gains in resonance as the century runs out. W. H. Auden, who was first and foremost a poet, succeeded in combining in his work the two classic pursuits: beauty and truth; and in his diction he brought together the lofty and the commonplace. While he was rooted in his age, his cadences survive and flourish beyond his own, only too brief, lifespan.

The Berg Collection is the proud possessor of Auden's largest literary archive, from his earliest poetic compositions, written in the by now familiar foolscap ledger notebooks, to some of his best mature work in prose and verse. The Collection's Auden Papers are the most voluminous and important source of material on the poet on either side of the Atlantic. It seemed appropriate to publish this volume which contains poems of the poet's earliest period. The facsimile and transcription into type and the enlightening notes will allow the broader public the pleasures of reading that which only specialists and Auden's closest circle might otherwise enjoy. From 1963 to the present the Berg Collection made itself responsible to acquire whatever Auden manuscripts were obtainable either by purchase or gift. For all those opportunities, and especially to our generous donors, we and future generations are always going to be grateful. It is time that we express thanks again in print at the opening of this majestic volume, in particular to the generous friend of the Berg Collection who made this publication possible, William Jovanovich. Those of us who became more intimately acquainted with Auden's poetry could do no better than to speed this volume on its way with Auden's words written in memory of W. B. Yeats:

> For poetry makes nothing: it survives
> In the valley of its making where executives
> Would never want to tamper, flows on south
> From ranches of isolation and the busy griefs,
> Raw towns that we believe and die in; it survives,
> A way of happening, a mouth.[2]

LOLA L. SZLADITS
Curator, Berg Collection

---

1   "In Memory of Sigmund Freud" (*Collected Poems* The Franklin Library 1980 [*CP2*], 221).
2   "In Memory of W. B. Yeats" (*CP2*, 199–200).

Introduction

THE FORTUNES OF this battered blue ledger, now the first of W. H. Auden's working notebooks to be entirely reproduced in a facsimile edition, dramatize the changes in status that "classic" authors and their poems undergo. Those fortunes also imply the duties and temptations of an author's readers. The story begins, of course, with the lonely act of composition. Throughout his writing-life, Auden made regular use of large, solid, bound notebooks and many—though probably a small proportion of their total number—have survived. They had, for Auden, both an elevated and a mundane aspect, being variously a vault for the newly achieved poem, and a convenient workshop where he could chip away at the drafts, cancelled versions, re-workings, and adjustments which preceded what he finally considered a finished work. Very often, as here, a volume begun with one purpose in mind was gradually pressed into the opposite role, only, later, to be pressed back again. Auden's habit was to write at first only on the recto of each leaf, leaving the verso of the preceding leaf blank for whatever annotations or revisions he might want to make. Thus none of these ledgers can simply be read straight through, like a printed book. Because a revision cannot, usually, be dated, the sequence of events must remain general and indefinite. When was "sweet" made "breathed" (p [51])? The facts are there under our eyes, but we cannot order them with any precision.

The notebook presented here dates from that crucial period at, and just after, Oxford, which Auden later judged to be the threshold of his mature career. It was a typical spell of ambition and anxiety, that began with T. S. Eliot's rejection on behalf of Faber and Faber of the collection that Auden submitted to him in June 1927, and ended with Eliot's acceptance of an entirely different collection sometime in the late spring of 1930. This notebook is particularly rich in both private and public significance for Auden's solidifying identity as a poet. It contains, amongst many other poems, his fair copy of "The Watershed" (p [37]), composed after a journey to Yugoslavia with his father in the summer of 1927. This is the first work that Auden judged was written entirely in his own "voice." The notebook also holds many of the lyrics which, during 1928, Auden suddenly felt "to be part of something" and which coalesced in his charade *Paid on Both Sides*. This strange, passionate drama, when it appeared in Eliot's *Criterion* in January 1930, brought Auden before an influential public for the first time.

Much of the facsimile's initial interest will be of a fascinatingly occult kind. It derives from the opportunity of watching how, in a famous poem like "The Watershed," the familiar, defining lineaments emerged as scrawled revisions to a now utterly foreign original. Thus the line "Stranger, turn back again, frustrate and vexed," authoritative and inevitable as it now seems, in fact only appeared at the last moment, as Auden's frustrated rummaging with "non-plussed" and "frozen" eventually yielded to the Hardyesque "frustrate."

The second of the emblematic changes which this notebook illustrates, some twenty years and many thousands of lines on, is the antithesis to that initial struggle for life. On Christmas Eve 1949, in the glow of mid-career, Auden, who was now settled in New York and a famous public man surrounded by peers and admirers, gave the notebook to Alan Ansen, a distinguished pupil. Mr Ansen occasionally performed secretarial and literary tasks for the poet, and he suggests that once the notebook had lost its potential as a quarry for works-in-progress Auden may have seen it as a nice reward for Ansen's labours. Indeed, it does seem that around this time Auden had been indulging in a phase of artistic retrospection. In *The Age of Anxiety*, his "baroque eclogue" published in 1947, Rosetta, the persona representing Feeling in Auden's Jungian scheme, reviews (through a rococo lens) her pre-war English childhood. Then, after completing this closet drama, Auden for a while contemplated a long work, to be called *Underground Life*, which would be focussed on the world of the miners in that scarred Northern landscape described in his poems of twenty years before. In this sense, relinquishing the notebook may have signalled Auden's intention to put this phase behind him. Auden maintained that one of the "chapters" in his life began in 1948 when he first rented a summer house on Ischia. The new tone in his poems was ripe, more relaxed and meditative. As it turned out, his next large-scale work was, indeed, a cycle of poems about landscapes, "Bucolics," but the treatment had become less localized and far more conceptual.

At some unknowable time in those twenty-odd years before the book was given away, fifty-five leaves were torn or excised from it. It is now impossible to determine exactly what was on most of those pages, or when they were removed, and why this happened. There is, however, no reason to believe that any poems were actually lost as a result: plenty of poems not found in this notebook but dating from the same period exist in other manuscripts. There are more than enough of these to fill up the missing pages, and it seems unlikely that Auden would have felt that a poem had reached a sufficiently advanced stage to be inscribed here, and not, as was his almost invariable habit, also have sent copies of it to his friends.

In 1975, two years after Auden's death, the notebook's third transition, the stage of which this facsimile is a part, began. Mr Ansen gave the volume to the Henry W. and Albert A.

Berg Collection of The New York Public Library, where today it constitutes an important part of the Library's uniquely rich Auden holdings. This third phase is a new beginning. Individuals' memories of Auden the man are now starting to gutter. His manuscripts have been scattered from Scotland to Texas on the financial winds, and new generations of readers are coming to him, each with a further diminished sense of Auden's old semi-mythical status. Inexorably, he is changing into language and a body of work. Correspondingly, as this facsimile should remind us, "the words of a dead man / Are modified in the guts of the living."

In a circuitous way, then, this prospect of a long, continually modifying future into which Auden the canonical author is now plunging brings us back to the young man on the verge of becoming "W. H. Auden." For textual work, nothing can substitute for close examination of the notebook itself, but as an aid to the study of Auden's compositional methods, as a clear record of the vagaries by which what we are now tempted to read as natural and fixed actually came into being, and as a reminder that a vast amorphous written background haunts each separate poem, then this facsimile, together with Patrick Lawlor's transcription, will be a valuable resource.

"Am I really so obscure?" Auden asked Naomi Mitchison after *Poems* (1930) was published. Although, as times change, different parts of the *oeuvre* will continue to fall in and out of focus, much has already been done to see beyond the supposedly impenetrable surface of Auden's early poems. Indeed, no other stretch of his work has yet been so carefully and minutely examined. This is, in part, because these are the poems most amenable to the psychologically based critical tradition with its eye on conflict and ambivalence from which Auden himself emerged. (Later on, the crack separating Auden's poems from contemporary critical methods became a gulf.) Certainly, during the nearly two years when Auden was using this notebook, he suffered an adult's share of emotional and circumstantial uncertainty, including several failed love affairs, a period of self-inflicted celibacy, an engagement (later broken off), an ignominious end to his university career at Oxford, an unsuccessful psychoanalysis, a break with England in October 1928 when he went to live in Berlin, and an almost complete revolution in his view of human nature. The factual details have all been amply laid out in Humphrey Carpenter's *W. H. Auden: A Biography* (1981).

Although the buried progress of Auden's development as a poet cannot be fitted exactly to such narrative highs-and-lows, his careful record of date and place for each composition demonstrates that he did conceive of the poems—at least afterwards—in occasional, circumstantial terms. More generally, Auden's annotations in the early pages of this notebook, whether concerned to fix an inspiration or to bring out a source, conceal an editorializing, distancing impulse.

The drama of his struggle to find his own poetic identity, as work by Katherine Bucknell will soon show, was actually a battle waged obscurely with the looming presences of his immediate poetic ancestors—Hardy, Yeats, Eliot—rather than with those distant, neutralized writers he picks out in his notes here: the nameless Anglo-Saxons, Prudentius, or Spenser. Auden kept up, to a greater or lesser extent, this practice of pointing out minor allusions or locating famous poems within a biographical context throughout his life, whenever he got hold of friends' copies of his books. In fact, he seems to have been almost constitutionally unwilling to discuss the real nature of his own writing, unless under the guise of a statement about someone or something else. Then, as his preface to *The Protestant Mystics* (1964), for example, shows, he could be radiantly explicit. In any case, the arcana picked up at university can easily, as they were perhaps subconsciously intended to, divert the attention from the strong, guilt-ridden emotions at the core of these magnificent poems.

Turning through the pages of this facsimile, it becomes clear that the process of Auden's revisions was more complex than the smooth hilarity of Christopher Isherwood's account in *Lions and Shadows* can accommodate. As the narrator of the book has it:

> If I wanted an adjective altered, it was altered then and there. But if I suggested that a passage should be rewritten, [Wystan] would say: 'Much better scrap the whole thing,' and throw the poem, without a murmur, into the waste-paper basket. If, on the other hand, I had praised a line in a poem otherwise condemned, then that line would reappear in a new poem. And if I didn't like this poem, either, but admired a second line, then both the lines would appear in a third poem, and so on—until a poem had been evolved which was a little anthology of my favourite lines strung together without even an attempt to make connected sense.

Once he was past his Eliot-influenced phase, which just preceded the time when he began to use this notebook, Auden's efforts as he went over his poems were not intended to make the lines more and more securely hermetic, but to clarify a poem's structure. So, in what eventually became the final chorus to *Paid on Both Sides*, the poem beginning here "But he is defeated," the original version (p [67]) carries inside it three stanzas—the second, third, and fifth—that blur what we can now recognize as an authentically Audenesque mood of grand, tragic calm. All the details in the final version, most of which is copied onto the preceding page, are clear and integrated into the whole. However, the earlier draft contains several off-key misplaced lines: "He has tasted good, and what is it? / The White Wyandot is a fine hen." (These lines provide a good example of the distance between Auden's learning and the emotional centre of his poems at this time.) The conflicting voices here, some echoing that earlier Eliotic period, are ruthlessly and hygienically squeezed out in revision. It is a convincing illustration of Auden's later distinctions between perfect verbal and civil orders:

> A society which was really like a poem and embodied all the esthetic values of beauty, order, economy, subordination of detail to the whole effect, would be a nightmare of horror, based on selective breeding, extermination of the physically or mentally unfit, absolute obedience to its Director, and a large slave class kept out of sight in cellars.

(*Poets at Work* [1946] p 178)

If Auden was able to develop from his experience in the poetic workshop a critique of literary authoritarianism, another result was, towards the end of his career, his formulation of a parallel belief in the inability of any verbal system fully to embody the order it seeks. Using his own version of Paul Valéry's dictum that a poem is never completed (an impossible state) but only abandoned (the actual state), whether through lack of time or the pressure of other obligations, or because another poem begins to form in the poet's mind, Auden began to envisage his works as infinitely pliable *after* publication as well as before it. In his case, there was a special necessity for such a rationale, since he had to justify the older Christian poet's straightening and correcting of the younger man's more anarchic productions. However, in the present context, the notion is a reminder of the dual virtues of persistence and abnegation which the poet must cultivate. Auden certainly knew when to hammer at what had initially seemed done. The poem which started out with "He, the trained spy, had walked into the trap" (p [69]) is an obvious case. Rapidly or not, it is hard to say, this mutated into the text his audience has always known: "Control of the passes was, he saw, the key." However, the facsimile also offers many examples of Auden's talent for knowing when to let go. Nothing except a spurious sense of a poem's inevitability could prepare the reader for the release of the final line in "Because sap fell away" (p [51]), when "sweet" metamorphosed into "breathed": "a breathed surrender."

For the literary critic, though, Valéry's formula emphasizes that a great deal of his chosen author's manuscript material will remain secondary to the real elucidatory task. This facsimile is really just an adjunct to the poems as Auden's present and future readers will have them, in editions based on texts that, in one manner or another, went public. There, like the peninsula in Auden's "Spain," each is a "fragment nipped off" from a larger chaos, and has become a place where "Our fever's shapes are precise and alive." Of the point at which *that* transition occurs, the poet himself is always the first judge.

Nicholas Jenkins

The Notebook:

Facsimile and Transcription

Freud

    Group Psychology

    Case Histories

    Papers on Metapsychology.

Social Basis of Consciousness   Burrow

Crime as Custom   } in savage society }

Sex as an Offence   } Malinowski

Sexual life of savages.   Rivers

    Gestalt.   Koffka

Freud[1]
      Group Psychology
     Case Histories
   Preface or Metapsychology.

Social Basis of Consciousness   Burrows[2]
Crime and Custom⌐
Sex and Repression⌐   in savage society⌐
Sexual Life among Savages   Mali   Malinowski[3]
Gestalt.   Koffka[4]

1/3[5]

W. H. <u>Auden.</u>

Poems.

~~March~~ ~~May 1927–~~ May 1927–March 1929.

W.H. Auden.

Poems.

~~March May 1927~~ — May 1927 - March 1929.

Amoeba in the running water
Lives afresh as son and Daughter.
"The Sword above the valley"
Said the worm to the penny.

a)   The sprinkler on the lawn   (For T. B A)
    weaves a cool vertigo, and stumps are drawn;
    The last boy vanishes,
    A blazer half-on, through the rigid trees.

b) Bones wrenched, weak whimper, lids wrinkled, first dazzle known,
    world-wonder hardened as bigness, years, ~~things~~ would knowledge, you.
    Make ~~presence~~ Presence smell a rich mould augured for roots urged, but gone
    ~~[...]~~
    ~~which ... began ... So flesh dough fills up ... to spelling~~
    ~~... spirit. So ... ~~
    The soul is tetanus; gun-barrel varnishing
    In summer grass, mind his to tarnish, untouched, enduring
    Though body stir to sweat, or squat as wily, hood,
    Infuriate the fire with bellows, blank till sleep
    feed two-faced dream. 'I want' voices, treble as once
    Crudely through flowers till dunghill cock-crow, crack at East.
    Eyes, unwashed jewels, the glass floor shipping, feel, knew Day,
    life stripped to girders, monochrome. Decent of instinct,
    Feature, figure, form irrelevant, dismissed, ~~Ought passes~~
    Ought passes through points fair-plotted, and you can form,
    seen yes or no. Before which argument my life are impudent.

c) The Megalopsych, says Aristotle
    Never runs swinging his arms.
    So when I saw the Reverend Bythesea Bubb   Rcin.
    The customary fine for frivolity was inflicted
    But when I was drunk, "Goo Goo" I says
    'Lovely men."

S̶ ̶E̶d̶m̶u̶n̶d̶s̶.̶ [1]

Amoeba in the running water[2]
Lives afresh as son and daughter.
"The sword above the valley"
Said the worm to the penny.

T̶h̶e̶ ̶p̶a̶u̶c̶i̶ "Paucity that never was simplicity" Owen. Insensibility[3]

1   a) ~~The sprinkler on the lawn~~[2]   (For J. B A)[p/i1]
        ~~Weaves a cool vertigo, and stumps are drawn;~~ ←
        ~~The last boy vanishes,~~
        ~~A blazer half-on, through the rigid trees.~~

        ————

    b) Bones wrenched, weak whimper, lids wrinkled, first dazzle known,[3]
                                    brought
        World-wonder hardens/ed as bigness, years, ~~br~~ ~~brings~~ knowledge, you.
                Presence
        ~~Rank a presence~~—smell a rich mould augurs/ed for roots urged, but [p/i] gone[p/i]
        [~~Eased by mucous tenderness to absorb the work~~— [p/i]
                                    fills up
        ~~Which was before began/begun: so flesh dough suffits to spilling~~ [p/i]   [5]
        ~~Concave of spirit. So you here I here] but gone~~ [p/i]
        The soul is tetanous; gun-barrel burnishing
        In summer grass, mind lies to tarnish, untouched, undoing   5
        Though body stir to sweat, or, squat as idols, brood,
        Infuriate the fire with bellows, blank till sleep   [10]
        And two-faced dream. 'I want' voiced, treble as once
        Crudely through flowers till dunghill cock-crow, crack at East.
        Eyes, unwashed jewels, the glass floor slipping, feel, know Day,   10
        Life stripped to girders, monochrome. Deceit of instinct,
        Feature, figure, form, irrelevant, dismissed, ~~Ought passes/d~~   [15]
        Ought passes through points fair-plotted, and you conform,
        Seen yes or no. Before which argument my buts are impudent.

        ————

    c) The Megalopsych, says Aristotle[4]
        Never runs swinging his arms.
        So when I saw the Reverend Bythesea Bubb   Rain.
        The customary fine for paucity was inflicted ←
        But when I was drunk. "Goo Goo' I said   5
        'Lovely men."

written 8 August 1926.

"Daffodil bulbs instead of eyes"   Eliot. _Sweeney among_
                                            the colours of mortality

written autumn 1923.

written 8 August 1926.

"Daffodil bulbs instead of eyes"   Intimations
                                      Eliot. ~~Whispers~~ of Mortality[1]

written Autumn. 1923.

[PAGE 8: facing page removed]

No trenchant parting this   ~~1~~
Of future from the past,
No idol fractured is
Nor bogey scared at last.
Yet still the mind will tease   5
In local irritation,
And difficult images
Demand an explanation.
Across this finite space
~~Nourished expensively~~ [P/i] Buttressed[P/i] expensively[P/i]   10
The pointed hand would place
Error in you, in me:
Eye squiny for a way
To mitigate the stare,
When shadow turns on day   15
Find argument too bare
    pendulum again:
Till ~~pendulums again~~ ~~morning over again~~
Restore the gravamen.
But standing now I see
The diver's brilliant bow[1]   20
His quiet break from the sea,
With one trained movement throw
The ~~hair~~ hair from his forehead.
And I, stung by the sun,
Think semi-satisfied,   25
That ere the smile is done
The eye deliberate
May qualify the joy
And that which we create
We also may destroy.   30

Dubrovnik.[2] August 1927

No trenchant parting this
Of future from the past,
No icod fractured is
Nor vaguely scarred at last.
Yet still the mind will tease
In local irritation,
And difficult images
Demand an explanation.

From this finite space
~~Resist expressly~~ Buttresses expensively
The pointed hand works free
Error in you, in me:
Eye syring for a way
To instigate the stare,
When shadow turns onday
Find argument to bare
~~Kindula~~ again:
Till ~~position again~~ ~~~~~~~~~~~~~~
Restore the gravamen.

But standing now I see
The diver's brilliant bar
His quiet break from the sea,
With one trained movement throw
The ~~long~~ hair from his ~~forehead~~.
And I, stung by the sun,
Think semi-satisfied
That ere the smile is done
The eye deliberate
May qualify the joy
And that which we create
We also may destroy.

                    Dubrovnik. August 1927

Who stands, the crux left of the watershed,
On the wet road between the chafing grass,
Below him sees dismantled washing-floors,
Snatches of tramline ~~banked up from the stream~~. running to the wood
An industry already comatose.   5

Yet sparsely living. A ramshackle engine
At Cashwell raises water; for ten years
It lay in flooded workings until this,
       latter
Its ~~second~~ office, grudgingly performed.
And further here and there, though many dead   10
Lie under the poor soil, some acts are chosen
Taken from recent winters. Two there were
Cleaned out a damaged shaft by hand, clutching
The winch the gale would tear them from; one died,
During a storm, the fells impassable,   15
Not at his village:—in his wooden shape
Through long abandoned levels nosed his way
And in a final valley went to ground.

Go home now stranger, proud of your young stock;
                          frustrate ~~frozen frustrate~~ ℓℓ
Stranger, turn back again, ~~non-plussed~~ and vexed.   20
This land, cut-off, will not communicate,
Be no accessory content to one:
Aimless for faces rather there than here.
Beams from your car may cross a bedroom wall,
They wake no sleeper. You may hear the wind   25
Arriving, driven from the ignorant sea
To hurt itself on pane, or bark of elm
Where sap unbaffled rises, being Spring.
But seldom this. Near you, taller than grass
Ears poise before decision, scenting danger.   30

Harborne¹ August 1927.

Who stands, the crux left of the watershed,
On the wet road between the chafing grass,
Below him sees dismantled washing-floors,
Snatches of tramline ~~banked up from the stream~~, running to the wood
An industry already comatose.

Yet sparsely living. A ramshackle engine
At Cashwell raises water; for ten years
It lay in flooded workings until this,
Its latter office, grudgingly performed.
And further here and there, though many dead
Lie under the poor soil, some acts are chosen
Taken from recent winters. Two there were
Cleaned out a damaged shaft by hand, clutching
The winch the gale would tear them from; one died,
During a storm, the fells impassable,
Not at his village: — in his wooden shape
Through long abandoned levels nosed his way
And in a final valley went to ground.

Go home now stranger, proud of your young stock;
Stranger, turn back again, frustrate ~~and cross and~~ and cross.
This land, cut-off, will not communicate,
Be no accessory content to one;
Aimless for faces rather there than here.
Beams from your car may cross a bedroom wall,
They wake no sleeper. You may hear the wind
Arriving, driven from the ignorant sea
To hunt itself on frame, on bark of elm
Where sap unbaffled rises, being spring;
But seldom this. Near you, taller than grass
Ears poise before decision, scenting danger.

Harborne August 1927.

Suppose they met, the inevitable procedure
Of hand to nape would drown the staling cry
Of cuckoos, filter off the day's detritus
And breach in their continual history.

Yet, spite of this new heroism, they feared   5
That doddering Jehovah whom they mocked.
Enough for him to show them to their rooms.
They slept apart though doors were never locked.

[The womb began its crucial expulsion.
The fishermen, aching, drenched to the skin,   10
The ledge cleared, dragged their boat up on the beach.
The survivor dropped, the bayonets closing in.]

In these, who saw, and never rubbed an eye,
A thousand dancers brought to sudden rest,
Transformed to tiger-lilies by the band,   15
It was no wonder they were not impressed

By certain curious carving in the porch
A generous designation of the fate
                    shut altogether from
Of those, ~~never involved in~~ P/i ~~a salvation.~~ shut altogether from salvation
Down they fell. Sorrow they had after that.   20

———

Carr Bridge.¹ September 1927.

Suppose they met, the inevitable procedure
Of hand to nape would drown the staling cry
Of cuckoos, filter off the day's detritus
And break in their continual history.

Yet, spite of this new heroism, they feared
That doddering Jehovah whom they mocked.
Enough for him to show them to their rooms.
They slept apart though doors were never locked.

[The wound began its crucial expulsion.
The fishermen aching, drenched to the skin,
The bilge cleared, dragged their boat up on the beach.
The survivor dropped, the bayonets closing in.]

In these, who sang and never rubbed an eye,
A thousand dancers brought to sudden rest,
Transformed to tiger-lilies by the band,
It was no wonder they were not impressed

By certain curious carving in the porch
A generous designation of the fate
Of those, ~~shut altogether from salvation~~ shut altogether from salvation
Down they fell. Sorrow they had after that.

Carr Bridge. September 1927.

Nox, et tenebrae, et nubila
confusa mundi et turbida,
lux intrat, albescit polus,
Christus venit, discedite.

Prudentius. Cath. II l. 1-4.

c.f. Spenser. Faery Quee: "not perceable by anie starre. ..

The crowing of the cock
Though it may scare the dead
Call on the fire to strike
Such the yawning cloud
Shall also summon up
The pointed crocus top
  Which, smelling of the mould
    Breathes of the underworld.

The god was slain for love
The god was brought to birth
There in the sunless grave
Not pierceable by star
Nor spidery moonlight, where
The was many startle us
Back from her faul nest with
A solitary curse.

  The chosen in a cave
  Forgot old whiffs, chose
  Suffered the dizzy calm,
  Waited the rising storm,
  Prayed through the searching season,
  And ~~say~~ saw, ere daylight set,
  Blocked conducts in spite
    Debatable horizon.

Nox, et tenebrae, et nubila
   confusa mundi et turbida,
lux intrat, albescit polus,
   Christus venit, discedite.

                        Prudentius. Cath. II l. 1–4.[1]

     Cf. Spenser. Faery Queen. "Not pierceable by anie starre . .[2]

The crowing of the cock ②←
Though it may scare the dead
Call on the fire to strike
Sever the yaw[n]ing cloud
Shall also summon up   5
The pointed crocus top
Which, smelling of the mould,
Breathes of the underworld.

The god was slain for love
The god was brought to birth   10
There in the sunless grove
Not pierceable by star←
Nor spidery moonlight, where
A/The crow may startle us
Back from her foul nest with   15
A solitary curse.

The chosen in a cave
Forgot old whiffs, alive
Suffered the dizzy calm,
Waited the rising storm,   20
Prayed through the scorching season,
And say saw, ere daylight set,
Blocked conduits in spate
Delectable Horizon.

[cont. on p 43]

..... "der liebende psychogoge" Thomas Mann, Tod und Venedig.

ן

nvml

venoften. Anabasis.

"when the doors being shut...for fear of the Jews." St John XX . 19.

Such kept back since, done with;
The tired ears prick, and beg
For altered pressure; eyes
Look in the glass, confess
The tightening of the mouth,
Know the receding face
A blemished psychogogue:
But symmetry will please,

Now straightly swallowed up
In memory like these
Its tilting planes decline
— The snowstorm in the marsh,
The champagne at the lips —
Swung into vision, fresh
By fleeting contact. Mind
Sees finally outlined

To breast the final hill
'θάλασσα' on the tongue,
Snap at the dragon's tail
To find the yelp its own;
Or sit, the doors being shut,
'Twixt coffee and the fruit;
Touching, decline to hear
Sounds of conclusive war.

Carr Bridge. September. 1929.

. . . . . "der liebende psychogogue."   Thomas Mann.   Tod und Venedig.[1]

Xenophon.   Anabasis.[2]

                       were
When "The doors ~~being~~ shut . . . . for fear of the Jews."   § John XX. 19.[3]

Such kept back since, done with;   25
The tired ears prick, and beg
An altered pressure; eyes
Look in the glass, confess
The tightening of the mouth,
Know the receding face   30
A blemished psychogogue:←
But symmetry will please.

Now straightly swallowed up
In memory like these
Its tilting planes disclose   35
—The snowstorm in the marsh,
The champagne at the lip—
Swung into vision, fresh
By fleeting contact. Mind
Sees faculty confined   40

To breast the final hill
'Θαλασσα' on the tongue,←
Snap at the dragon's tail
To find the yelp its own;
Or sit, the doors being shut,←   45
'Twixt coffee and the fruit;
Touching, decline to hear
Sounds of conclusive war.

Carr Bridge. September. 1927

Þonne onwæcneð eft winelēas guma
gesihð him biforan fealwe wēgas
baþian brimfuglas.   The Wanderer 45-47

Syllic wæs se sigebēam,   and ic synnum fāh.
                                        Dream of the rood 13.

                                   level
Boys and girls are equal now with men.   Antony and Cleopatra IV 13.

cf. Ezekiel XXXVII v. 3.

Nor was that final, for about that time
Gannets, blown over northward, going home,
Surprised the secrecy beneath the skin.

". Wonderful was that cross and I full of sin":
"- Approaching, utterly generous, came one
For years expected, born only for me".

Returned from that dishonest country, we
Awake, yet tasting the delicious lie,
And boys and girls, {equal} to be, are different still.

No, these bones shall live while daffodil
And saxophone have something to recall
Of Man's bone and of the wounded heel.

Harborne. October 1927.

ðonne onwæcneð eft   winelēas guma
gesihð him biforan   fealwe wǣgas
baþian brimfuglas.   The Wanderer 45–47[1]

Syllic wæs se sigebēam,   and ic synnum fāh.
                              Dream of the rood l. 13.[2]

                    level.
Boys and girls are equal now with men.   Antony and Cleopatra IV 13.[3]

cf. Ezekiel XXXVII v. 3.[4]

Nor was this/at final, ~~the~~ for about this/at time
Gannets, blown over northward, going home,
Surprised the secrecy beneath the skin.⬅

—"Wonderful was that cross and I full of sin."⬅
—"Approaching, utterly generous, came one   5
For years expected, born only for me."

Returned from that dishonest country, we
Awake, yet tasting the delicious lie,
And boys and girls, ⌈~~level~~ equal⌉
⌊~~equal~~⌋ to be, are different still.⬅

No, these bones shall live while daffodil⬅   10
And saxophone have something to recall
Of Adam's brow and of the wounded heel.

                    Harborne. October 1927.

Deemed this an outpost, I
The exiled governor,
Myself a photograph
In mittens on the snow
To write home once a year
Watching the last leaf fall.

At vigil heard approach
The old and twilight foe,
Experienced, to this
Deliberately come:
But 'neath Beneath my supple grip
There was no entire vow;

Scales wriggled into flesh
Of a more yielding week,
Glare fading from the eye &
Left limp within the arms
Your new and sensible
Assertive innocence.

Then at the Hall all night
The babble of the flute
The inarticulate cello
Held insolent revel
To testify at last
The destined requiem.

Deemed this an outpost, I
The exiled governor
Myself a photograph
In mittens on the snow
To write home once a year   5
Watching the last leaf fall.[1]

At vigil heard approach
The old and twilight foe,
                          for
Experienced a/to this
Deliberately come: 10
But 'neath ~~Beneath~~ my supple grip
There was no contrite roar.

Scales wriggled into flesh
Of a more yielding neck,
Glare fading from the eye   15
Left limp within the arms
Your new and sensible
Assertive innocence.

Then at the Hall all night
The babble of the flute   20
And inarticulate 'cello
Held insolent revel
To testify at last
The destined regiment.

Because sap fell away,   (For G. C.)[P/i1]
~~Cold's~~ Before cold's night attack~~s~~, we ~~saw?~~/see
A harried vegetation:
Upon our failure come
          lower
Down ~~In~~ To the ~~perpetual~~ changing room,   5
Honours on pegs, cast humours, we sit, lax,
In close ungenerous intimacy,
Remember
Falling in slush, shaking hands
With a snub-nosed winner;[2]   10
Open a random locker, sniff with distaste
          mouldy[P/i]
At a ~~fly-blown~~[3] passion.

Love, is this love, that notable forked-one,
Riding away from the farm, the ill word said,
Fought at the frozen dam?[4] Who prophesied   15
Such lethal factors, understood
The indolent ulcer?[5] Brought in now
Love lies at surgical extremity;
~~The bowls prepared, the rubber gloves assumed,~~
          breathed
Gauze pressed over the mouth, a ~~sweet~~ surrender.   [20]

                    Oxford. November 1927.

(For G.C.)

Because sap fell away
~~Colo's~~ Before cold's night attacks, we see
Of hurried vegetation:
When our failure come
To the ~~perpetual~~ changing room,
Honours on pegs, cast humours, we sit, let,
In close ungenerous intimacy,
Remember
Falling in slush, shaking hands
With a snub-nosed winner;
Open a random locker, smell with distaste
Of a ~~flyblown~~ mouldy passion.

Love, is this love, that notable forked-one,
Riding away from the farm, the ill word said,
Fought at the frozen dam? Who prophesies
Such lethal factors, understood
The indolent ulcer? Brought in now
Love lies at surgical extremity;
The bandage prepares, the rubber gloves assumed,
Gauze pressed over the mouth, a ~~sweet~~ breathed surrender.

Oxford. November 1927.

He let his pane of handow before Margin
Havoc wip pass holtes ans to patue hise slch.

This the advent of the lost soul
To the lost body —

　　　　　　" That was all
Cancelled original light, secured
A sour union, not preferred.

Often, equipped and early, you
Traced figures in the dust, eager
To start, but on the edge of some
So often them refused me farther;

　　　　　　with
Disarming me ~~with~~ the concussion
Of lamp and violin and passion,
Offered a real image, fresh,
Constant to every loyal nick.

　Plumes the straining
~~Let~~ not the ~~quarry~~ hawk ~~fly to the~~ wood
Though quarry mocked at him
Near to the Dark Tower's cave
But turning at the Hill crest, head.

He let him þare of handon   lēofne flēogan
Havoc wiþ þæs holtes   and to þǣre hilde stop.[1]

This the address of the lost soul
To the lost body—
                      "That was ill
~~S~~/Cancelled original light, secured
A sour union, not preferred.

Often, equipped and early, you   5
Traced figures in the dust, eager
To start, but on the edge of snow
As often then refused me farther;

              ~~by~~ with
Disarming me ~~with~~ the concussion
Of lamp and violin and passion,   10
Offered a real image, fresh,
Constant to every loyal wish.

  Plumed the straining
~~Let not~~ the ~~quarry~~ hawk ~~fly to the wood~~
         little   ~~moe~~
  Though ∧quarry mocked at him←
Never to the Dark Tower we came   15
    But turning at the Hill crest, heard.

This the address of the lost soul
To the lost body.

That was ill
Cancelled original light, secured
A sour union, not preferred.
Death's insulation now between
Saying that you no longer please
Love trespassing asked enjoys
The luxury of cooling love
Mind spoke into flesh the whole night through.

Often, equipped and early, you
Traced figures in the dust, eager
To start, but on the edge of snow
to often then refused me further;
Proffered a real visage, fresh,
Constant to every loyal wish.

Never to the Dark Tower we rode
But standing on the hill-crest, heard,
Catching the breath for the applause,
A tolling disillusion bell,
The leaking of an hour-glass
Till lightning loosed the frantic skull.

Granted that in a garden once
And a wind blowing, a voice
Beyond the wall, unbroken, tied
The jabber of the blood, and bred
No fever"

Cocks crew and sleeping men turned over.
Rain fell for miles, ghosts went away.
The faint of heart doubted, stopped at safety.

This the address of the lost soul
To the lost body—

                  That was ill
~~Cancelled original light,~~ secured
A sour union, not preferred.
Death's insulation now between   [5]
Sorry that you no longer please
Love trespassing apart enjoys
The luxury of cooling bone
Mind spoke with flesh the whole night through.
"Often, equipped and early, you   [10]
Traced figures in the dust, eager
To start, but on the edge of snow
As often then refused me further;   5
P[r]offered a real image, fresh,
Constant to every loyal wish.   [15]

Never to the Dark Tower we rode
But, standing on the hill-crest, heard,
Catching the breath for the applause,   10
A tolling disillusioned bell,
The leaking of an hour-glass   [20]
Till lightning loosed the frantic skull.[1]

Granted that in a garden once
And a wind blowing, a voice   15
Beyond the wall, unbroken, hid
The jabber of the blood, and bred   Cocks crew and sleeping men turned over.   [25]
No fever"   Rain fell for miles, ghosts went away.   20
                              The jaw, long-dropped, stopped at reply.

From the very first coming down
Into a new valley with a frown
Because of the sun and a lost way,
You certainly ~~rem~~ remain. To-day,
I, crouching behind a sheep-pen, heard   5
Travel across a sudden bird,
Cry out against the storm, and found
The year's arc a completed round,
And love's worn circuit rebegun,
Endless with no dissenting turn.   10
Shall see, shall pass, as we have seen
The swallow on the tile, Spring's green
                    shiver
Preliminary ~~giggle~~, passed
                    truck the
A solitary ~~waggon~~, last
Of shunting in the Autumn. But now,   15
To interrupt the homely brow,
Thought warmed to evening through and through,
Your letter comes, speaking as you
Speaking of much but not to come.

Nor
 ∧ Speech ~~is not~~/ is close ~~Teeth are not locked~~ nor fingers numb   20
If love not seldom has received
An unjust answer, was deceived.
I, decent with the seasons, move
Different or with a different love,
Nor question overmuch the nod,   25
The stone smile of this country god,
That never was more reticent
Always afraid to say more than it meant.[1]

Oxford Dec 1927.

From the very first coming down
Into a new valley with a frown
Because of the sun and a lost way,
You certainly remain. To-day,
I, crouching behind a sheep-pen, heard
Travel across a sudden bird,
Cry out against the storm, and found
The year's arc a completed round,
And love's worn circuit rebegun,
Endless with no dissenting turn.
Shall see, shall pass, as we have seen
The swallow on the tile, Spring's green
Preliminary shiver, passed
A solitary truck, the last
Of shunting in the Autumn. But now,
To interrupt the homely brow,
Thought warmed to evening through and through,
Your letter comes, speaking as you
Speaking of much but not to come.

Feeling are not numb nor fingers numb
If love not seldom has received
An unjust answer, was deceived.
I, decent with the seasons, move
Different or into a different love,
Nor question much, the nod,
The stone smile of this country god,
That never was more reticent
Always afraid to say more than it meant.

Oxford Dec 1927.

The Four sat on in the bare room
Together, and the fire unlighted,
One was speaking;—" She turned the page,
Here graves on the other side"....

Love parted in the waiting-room
Scraping back chairs for the wrong train."
Said Two; as Three   " All kinds of love
Are obsolete or extremely rare".

" On Yesterday', the last said, ' falling on me
The shadow of returning girls
Proclaimed an insolent new day, Spring
Quick. Newborn, and eagle above the pools."

Thus said the few distinguished men
Who sat, watching the enemy.
Saw, closing upon the bare room
The weight of a whole winter night,
And began the reef high-breaking surf.

                    The four sat on in the bare room
                    Together, and the fire unlighted,
One said, 'We played duets' ~~And one was speaking~~;—"She turned the page,
                    More quavers on the other side". . . .

              We "~~And~~ parted in the waiting-room   5
                    Scraping back chairs for the wrong train."[1]
Said Two; and Three ~~Another then~~ "All kinds of love
                    Are obsolete or extremely rare."

                              Four
                    "~~Th~~ Yesterday,' ~~the last~~ said, '~~To me~~ falling on me
                    The shadow of returning girls   Through the glass pavement overhead   [10] 10
                    Proclaimed ~~th~~ an insolent ~~new day~~, Spring   The shadow of returning girls
Quick. ~~New land, and eagles above the pools.~~"[2]   Proclaimed an insolent new Spring

                    Thus said the four distinguished men
                    Who sat, waiting the enemy,
                    Saw, closing ~~on~~/upon the bare room   15
                    The weight of a whole winter night,
                    ~~And~~ beyond the reef high-breaking surf.

[PAGE 58: rev. of p 59]

The four men sat in the

                              on
The Four ~~men~~ sat ~~down~~ in the bare room
         Together, and the fire unlighted,
         And one was speaking. "~~The page turned over~~   She turned the page
         More quavers on the other side. . . .

And ~~We~~ parted in a waiting-room   5
         Scraping back chairs for the wrong train."
         Another then—"All kinds of love
         Are obsolete or extremely rare."

         Yesterday   last ~~of turn~~
         '~~For my part~~' said the ~~next "I saw fall.~~ to me.
         "The shadow of returning girls   10
         Proclaimed an insolent new day
New land, ~~The~~ And eagles above the pools."

         Thus said the four distinguished men
         Who sat waiting the enemy
~~Who~~ ~~And~~ saw, closing upon the bare room   15
         The weight of a whole winter night
         And beyond the reef high-breaking surf.

———————————

Harborne. Dec 1927

~~The four men sat in the~~

Re.   Four ~~men~~ sat ~~down~~ in the bare room
       Together, and the fire unlighted,
   And one was speaking: "~~The page~~ ~~turns over~~ she turns the page
       More queens on the other side...."

And ~~the~~ perished in a waiting-room
       Scraping back chairs for the morning train:"
   Another then — "All kinds of love
       Are obsolete or extremely rare."

                 had after
   '~~Yesterday~~' ~~For the first~~ 'saw the ~~next~~ ~~"~~ ~~last fall~~ .' time.
   "The shadow of returning guilt
       Proclaimed an insolent new day
New law, ~~the~~ And eagles above the pools."

   Thus said the four distinguished men
   Who sat wanting the enemy
~~Who~~ ~~And~~ saw, closing upon the bare room
       The weight of a whole winter night
   And began the reef high-breaking surf.

———

                        Harborne. Dec 1927

The colonel to be shot at dawn
Plays a harmonium on the lawn.
Though stimulated by the tune
The subaltern will die in Tune.

Harborne Xmas Day 1927

The colonel to be shot at dawn
Plays a harmonium on the lawn.
Though stimulated by the tune
The subalterns[1] will die in June.

Harborne Xmas Day 1927.

a full

To-night, when ∧ storm surrounds the house

And the fire creaks, the many come to mind,

Sent forward in the thaw with anxious marrows. [i/P]

And Such a one, it seems, might now appear,   For such might now return, with a bleak face

returned

Might come in now, come back with a bleak face,   His hair cut off, and other messages   [5] 5

His hair cut off, and edified to know

That action has a rudimentary eye;

Tha What's felt at all, felt to extravagance,

Not adequate cause; the broken edge of fields   For a poor stimulant

Is tender still to movement

So, Almost seen   [10]

The image turns half lighted at the door,

A greater, but not fortunate in all.   10

Come back, deprived of an astonishing end

Morgan's who took a clean death in the North,

gale

Shouting against the wind, or Cousin Dodd's   [15]

Passed out, asleep in th her chair, the snow falling.

The too-loved clays borne over by diverse drifts,   15

Fallen upon the far side of all enjoyment,

move closer

Unable to Shall not be got/get together, shall not speak

that   stern

Out of the grave. To death, hard on no capital fault;   [20]

—Enough to have lightly touched the unworthy thing.

Harborne January 1928.

To-night, when a full storm surrounds the house

And the fire creaks, the many come to mind,

Sent forward in the thaw with anxious marrow.

~~Such a one, it seems, might now appear,~~   For such might now return, with a bleak face

~~By it come in now, returning into a bleak face,~~ His hair ... cut off, and other messages

~~the hair cut off, and ...~~

That action has a rudimentary eye;

~~For~~ What's felt at all, felt too extravagance,

~~The adequate cause, the hidden edge of pride~~   For a poor stimulant

~~Be tender still to movement~~

                                        So, Almost seen

Be image time half golldes at the door,

A greater, but not fortunate in all.

Sent back, refused of an astonishing end

Magnus who took a clean death in the Water,

Shouting, against the gale, or Cousin Dodds'

Pansed out, asleep in ~~the~~ her chair, the snow falling.

The two-lived days borne over by dwarise drifter,

Fallen upon the far side of all enjoyment,

Unable to ~~Start~~ ~~~~ never closer ~~get together~~, while at speed

Out of that grave. To ~~soothe~~ ~~stem~~ now are no capital fault;

    or caught to have lightly touched the unworthy thing.

                                        Harborne January 1928.

But he is defeated; let the son
Sell the farm, let the mountain fall;
His mother and her mother won.

His fields are used up when the moles visit
The contours worn flat; if there show
Passage for water, he will miss it,

Give up his breath, his woman, his team,
No life to touch, though later there be
Big fruit, eagles above the stream.

But he is defeated; let the son
Sell the farm, lest the mountain fall;
His mother and her mother won.

His fields are used up where the moles visit   5
The contours worn flat; if there show
Passage for water, he will miss it,

Give up his breath, his woman, his team,
No life to touch, though later there be
Big fruit, eagles above the stream.[1]

But he is defeated; let the son
Sell the farm, lest the mountain fall
His mother and her mother won.

Yes, he will come when the girls call
From the wood; he will step forward then   [5]
Out of the shadow of the wall.

Haemophilia is found in men.
He has tasted good, and what is it?[1]
The White Wyandot is a fine hen.

P /i

           are
His field/s ~~is~~ used up where the moles visit,   [10]
The contours worn flat: if there show   5
Passage for water he will miss it.

Confusion
~~Positions ar if~~ the judge think so
Become important; unless his seem
A comfortable answer he must ~~go;~~   [15]

          breath   woman
Give up his ~~ghost~~, his ~~wooing~~, his team;
No life to touch, though later there be
Big fruit, eagles above the stream.

London Jan. 1928.

But he is defeated; let the son
Sell the farm, lest the mountain fall
His mother and her mother won.

Yes, he will come when the girls call
From the wood; he will step forward then
Out of the shadow of the wall.

Haemophilia is found in men.
He has tasted good, and what is it?
The White Wyandot is a fine hen.

His fields are used up where the moles visit,
The contours worn flat: if there shed
Passage for water he will miss it.

                    Confusion
~~Borders~~ are if the judge thinks so
Become important; unless his seem
A comfortable answer he must go,

                    break
Give up his ~~gift~~, his ~~wooing~~ woman, his team;
No use to touch, though later there be
Big fruit, eagles above the stream.

                                        London Jan. 1928.

began

Control of the passes was the key, he thought, the guessed
To this new district, but who would get it
When the trained spy had walked into the trap,
For a bogus guide, seduced into the old tricks?

At greenhearth was a fine site for a dam
And easy power, had they pushed the rail
Some stations nearer; they ignored his wires,
The bridges were unbuilt and trouble coming

This street singer seemed gracious now to one,
For weeks up in the desert; woken by water
Running away in the dark, he often had
Reproached the night for a companion
Dreamed of already. They would shoot, of course,
Parting easily who were never joined.

                    he saw
Control of the passes was∧the key, he guessed
            fresh
To this new district, but who would get it
                the
When he,∧trained spy, had walked into the trap,
For a bogus guide, seduced with the old tricks?

At Greenhearth was a fine site for a dam[1]   5
And easy power, had they pushed the rail
Some stations nearer; They ignored his wires,
The bridges were unbuilt and trouble coming

                music
This street singer seemed gracious now to one,
For weeks up in the desert; woken by water   10
Running away in the dark, he often had
Reproached the night for a companion
Dreamed of already. They would shoot of course,
Parting easily who were never joined.[2]

[PAGE 68: rev. of p 69b]

He, the trained spy, had walked into the trap

~~Led by~~ ~~For a bogus guide~~ For a bogus guide, ~~de~~ seduced with the old tricks,

Control of the Passes was he saw the key

To this fresh district, but who would get it?

The work had been exciting, though it meant [5]

Continuous travel, sleeping in cottages

~~When~~ And he had often, woken by running water,

Reproached the night for a companion

Dreamed of already. They would shoot of course,

         were

~~Easil~~ Parting easily who ~~had~~ never joined. [10]

Control of the passes was, he saw, the key

To this fresh district, but who would get it?

He, the trained spy, had walked into the trap

For a bogus guide, seduced with the old tricks.

    business had its moments

The ~~work had been exciting~~ though it meant [5]

     for instance

Rough travelling,/: Woken by ~~running~~ water

Running away in the dark, he often had

Reproached the night for a companion

Dreamed of already. They would shoot of course

Parting easily who were never joined. [10]

Oxford. Jan 1928

He, the trained spy, had walked into the trap
~~too by~~ For a bogus guide, seduced into the old tricks,
Control of the passes was, he saw, the key
To this fresh district, but who would get it?
The work had been exciting, though it meant
Continuous travel / sleeping in cottages
~~when~~ he had often, woken by running water,
Reproached the night for a companion
Dreamed of already. They would shoot of course,
~~too~~ Parting easily who had never joined.

Control of the passes was, he saw, the key
To this fresh district, but who would get it?
He, the trained spy, had walked into the trap
For a bogus guide, seduced with the old tricks.
The ~~work had been exciting~~, though it meant
Rough travelling; Woken by ~~running~~ water
Running away in the dark, he often had
Reproached the night for a companion
Dreamed of already. They would shoot of course
Parting easily who were never joined.

Oxford. Jan 1928

Taller to-day, we remember similar evenings
Walking together in the windless orchard
Where the brook runs over the gravel, far from the glacier

Again in the room with the sofa hiding the grate
Look down to the river when the rain is over   5
      him
See ~~one~~ turn in the window, hearing our last
Of Captain Ferguson.[1]

It is seen how excellent hands have turned to commonness
One, staring too long, went blind in a tower
                              broke through and
One sold all his manors to fight, ~~but winning~~ trembled   10

                        the
~~The~~ n/Nights come bringing∧snow; and the dead howl
Under the headlands in their windy dwelling[2]
Because the Adversary put too easy questions
On lonely roads

But
~~But~~ happy now, though no nearer each other,   15
                        ~~the~~
                        a
~~Ea~~/We see the ~~bright lamps lit in farms up the valley~~ farms lighted
Down at the mill shed~~s~~ the hammering stops   all along the valley.
And men go home

Noises at dawn will bring
Freedom for some, but not this peace   20
No bird can contradict; passing, but is sufficient now
For something fulfilled this hour, loved or endured.

                        Oxford March 1928.

Taller to-day, we remember similar evenings
Walking together in the windless orchard
When the hook runs over the gravel, far from the glacier

Again in the room with the sofa hiding the grate
Look down to the river when the rain is over
See me turn in the window, hearing our last
Of Captain Ferguson.

It is seen how excellent hands have turned to common tasks
One, staring too long, went blind in a tower
One sold all his manor to fight, ~~broke through and~~ trembled

The ~~Myths~~ come buying the snow, and the dead howl
Under the headlands in their windy dwelling
Became the Adversary put too easy questions
On lonely roads

But
~~But~~ halfway now, though no nearer each other,
~~the~~ see the ~~light lamps lit~~ too ~~far up the valley~~ farms lighted
Down at the millsheds the hammering stops   all along the valley.
And men go home

Noises at dawn will bring
Freedom of some, but not this peace
No bird can contradict; passing, but is sufficient now
For something fulfilled this hour, loved or endured.

                                        Oxford March 1928.

The spring will come
Not hesitate for me enlarge who
Through a fine day and every pulley running
Would quickly lie down, nor save the wanted me
That, wounded in escaping, swam the lake
Safe to the reeds, collapsed in shallow water.

'You have tasted good and what is it? Be you
Sick in the green plain, healed in the tundra, shall
Turn westward back from your own success
Under a dwindling alp to see your friends
Cut down the wheat.

For where are Barley who won the Rim
Dutchmen so tasted by the House
Those who kept a sparrowhawk?
The clock strikes, it is time to go,
The tongue ashamed, deceived by a shake of the hand.

The Spring will come
Not hesitate for one employer who
Though a fine day and every pulley running
Would quick lie down, nor save the wanted one
That, wounded in escaping, swam the lake   5
Safe to the reeds, collapsed in shallow water.

You have tasted good and what is it?[1] For you
Sick in the green plain, healed in the tundra, shall
Turn westward back from your alone success
Under a dwindling alp to see your friends   10
Cut down the wheat.

For where are Basley who won the Ten
Dickon so tarted by the House
Thomas who kept a sparrowhawk?[2]
The clock strikes; it is time to go,   15
The tongue ashamed, deceived by a shake of the hand.

~~The summer quickens grass~~   There is a brilliant grass
~~Makes cover in the wood,~~   ~~A cave in the wood.~~
And many seek the good
Promised to them, and us.

Day after day is well
Hearing you speak; your eye
Meets mine, kind with a lie,
For neither can compel

                    The summer quickens grass   [5]
                    Scatters its promises
                    To you and me no less
                    Though neither can compel.

The wish to last the year,   5
The longest look to live,   [10]
The urgent word survive
The movement of the air.

But, loving now, let none
Think of divided days,   10
When we shall choose from ways,   [15]
All of them evil, one;

Look on with stricter brows
The sacked and burning town,
The ice-sheet moving down,   15
The fall of an old house.   [20]

Harborne. April 1928.

The summer quickens grass
Makes love in the wood,
And many seek the good
Promised to them, and us.

Day after day is well
Hearing you speak, your eye
Meets mine, kind into be,
For neither can compel

There is a brilliant grass
A leaf in the wood.

The summer quickens grass
Scatters its promises
To you and me no less
Though neither can compell.

The wish to last the year,
The longest look to live,
The urgent wad survive
The movement of the air.

But, loving now, let none
Think of divided days,
When we shall choose from ways,
All of them evil, one;

Look on with stricter brows
The sacked and burning town,
The ice-sheet moving down,
The fall of an old house.

Hartone. April 1928.

Grow thin by walking, and go inland,
He told himself, as the unmended road
Climbed higher and he left the birds behind.
Rocks had still shadows and his crossed them.
His long strides reached the pass by noon, and there   5
He found a shelter from the wind to doze in till
The easy four o'clock descent he made
Following a growing stream and passing no one[1]
Though one, nearer all day, turned suddenly
And left a clear path downhill to the station.   10
The line ran into cuttings either way,
Iron up valleys to a hidden village.[2]
There were two trains; he could return, or go
Further and learn some native ignorance
                                              explain
~~W.~~ No case from Belgium to ~~support~~ it by.[3]   15
"No need; love is not there" he said, for eyes
Looked only outward, and he chose his ~~eh~~ train
Till town lights welcomed him, and many people
To lie about the cost of a night's lodging.[4]
Later he fell asleep; proud of his day   20

Oxford. April 1928.

"Grow thin by walking, and go in afraid,"
he told himself, as the remainder road
Climbs higher and he left the birds behind.
Rocks have still shadows and his course to run.
His long stride reaches the pages by noon, and there
he found a shelter for the mind to doze in till
the easy farmsteads offered he made
following, growing slower and passing no one
Though on, nearer all day, times suddenly
he left a clear path down till to the station.
The line ran into cuttings after way,
Down up valleys to a hidden village.
There were two trains; he could return, or go.
fustian and lean sore native ignorance
too no cause for Belgium to support it by.
"No need; love is not there" he said, for eyes
looked only outward, and he chose his own train
Till town lights welcomed him, and many people
To lie about the cost of a night's lodging.
Later he fell asleep; proud of his day.

                          Oxford. April 1928.

Some say that handsome raider still at large
A terror to the marches in time is love:
And we must listen for such messengers
To tell us daily" To-day a scout came blessing
The links". " seen lately in the provinces
Reading behind a tree and people passing."

3

But love returns.
As once all hearts are turned this way, and love
Calls order – silences the angry sons –
Steps forward, greets, repeats what he has heard
And seen, feature for feature, word for word.

Some say that handsome raider still at large
A terror to the Marches in truth is love:
And we must listen t for such messengers
To tell us daily "To-day a saint came blessing
The huts." "seen lately in the provinces 5
Reading behind a tree and people passing."

But love returns.
At once all heads are turned this way, and love
Calls order—silenced the angry sons—
Steps forward, greets, repeats what he has heard 10
And seen, feature for feature, word for word.

Often the man, alone shut, shall consider
The killings in old winters, death of friends,
Sitting with stranger shall expect no good.[1]

There was no food in the assaulted city
Men spoke at corners, asking for news, saw   5
Outside the watchfires of a stronger army.

Spring came urging to ships, a casting-off
But one would stay, vengeance not done;[2] it seemed
Doubtful to them that they should meet again.

Fording in the cool of the day, they rode   10
To meet at crossroads when the year was over.
Dead is Brody. Such a man was Maul.

I will say this, not falsely: I have seen
The just and the unjust die in the day.
All, willing or not; and some were willing.   15

       July
    Hampstead. ~~June/Iy~~ 1928.

Often the man, alone shut, shall consider
The killings in old winters, death of friends,
Sitting with stranger shall expect no good.

There was no food in the assaulted city
Men spoke at corners, asking for news, saw
Outside the watchfires of a stronger army.

Spring came urging to ships, a casting-off
But one would stay, vengeance not done; it seemed
Doubtful to them that they should meet again.

Fading in the cool of the day, they rode
To meet at crossroads when the year was over.
Dead is Brody. Such a man was Mal.

I will say this, not falsely: I have seen
The just and the unjust die in the day.
All, willing or not; and some when willing.

Hampstead. July 1928.

To throw away the key and walk away
Not abrupt exile, the neighbours asking why,
                    a line
But following ~~a growing stream~~ with left and right, [1]
An altered gradient at another rate
Learns more than maps upon the whitewashed wall,   5
The hand put up to ask; and makes us well
Without confession of the ill. Bare to wind
It may examine but cannot unwind
Bandage of flesh [2] nor disguise the ~~bone~~ bane
Which has for some time now attacked the bone [3] —   10
Without   the
~~Nor~~ a set smile for guest~~s~~.; [~~for courage shifts~~
~~To who in alkali-fields~~ [4] ~~avoids the shafts,~~
~~Not to fatigued defiance.~~] All ~~the~~ pasts
Are single old past now although some posts
Are forwarded and reproduce the tang   [15]
Important once on the tip of the tongue,
Held in the hand and looking on a new view.   15
The future shall fulfil~~s~~ a surer vow,
Not smiling at queen over the glass-rim
Nor making gunpowder in the top-room.   [20]
Not promised to this, not to that. Know[ledge] shall increase.
Travelling up local lines shall come across   20
A variation on the ~~d~~/Dancing Boy
No case from Belgium to explain it by: [5]
Not swooping at the surface still like gulls   [25]
But with prolonged drowning shall develop gills. [6]

But there are still to tempt; areas not seen   25
Because of blizzards or an erring sign
Whose guessed-at wonders would be worth alleging,
And ~~lie~~ lies about the cost of a night's lodging [7]   [30]

[cont. on p 105]

To throw away the key and walk away

Not abrupt exile, the neighbours asking why,

But following a line ~~regarding steam~~ into left and right,

Finaltered gradient at another rate

Learns more than maps upon the whitewashed wall,

The hand first up to ask; and induces well

Without confession of the ill - Bare to wind

It may examine but cannot unwind

Bandage of flesh nor diagnose the ~~bone~~ bane

Which has for some time now attacked the bone —

~~Without~~   the

Nor a set smile for greeting; [for courage shifts

To other in alkali. fields invade the shales,

Not to fatigued defence.] Are ~~this~~ pasts

Are single old forest now although some pasts

Are forwarded and reproduce the tang

Important once on the lips of the tongue,

Held in the hand and looking on a new view.

The future shall fulfils a surer vow,

Not smiling at queen over the glass-rim

Nor making gunpowder in the tops-room,

Not promises to this, not to that, know shall increase,

Travelling up local lines still came across

A variation on the Dancing Boy

No case from Belgium to explain it by;

Not swooping at the surface still like gulls

But in the prolonged drowning shall develop gikes.

But there are still to tempt: areas not seen

Because of blizzards or an erring sign

Whose guessed-at wonders would be worth alledging;

And lies about the cost of a nightly lodging

Travellers may meet at inns but not attach;
They sleep one night together, not asked to touch,   30
Receive no normal welcome, not the pressed lip,
Children to lift, not the assuaging lap:
Crossing the pass descend the growing stream   [35]
Too tired to hear except the pulses strum,
Reach villages to ask for a bed in,   35
Rocks shutting out the sky, the old life done.

Spa.⁸ August 1928.

Travellers may meet at inns but not attach;
They sleep one night together, not asked to touch,
Receive no normal welcome, not the pressed lip,
Children to lift, not the assuaging lips:
Crossing the pass descend the growing stream
Too tired to hear except the pushes stream,
Reach villages to ask for a bed in,
Rocks shuttering and are shy, the old life done.

Spa. August 1928.

The Spring unsettles sleeping partnerships:

              upon

Foundries improve ~~upon~~ their ~~processes~~ process, and shops

Open a further wing on credit till

The winter. In summer boys grow tall

With running races on the wetted sand;   5

War is declared there~~;~~/, here a treaty signed;

Here a scrum breaks up like a bomb, there troops

Deploy like birds. But coming Autumn trips

Proudest. These gears which ran in oil for week

By ~~week,~~ week, needing no look, now will not work.   10

Those manors mortgaged twice to pay for love

Go to another.

              O how shall man live.

His thought born, child of one farcical night

To find him old. H~~is~~/e always breathes but not

By choice; he dreams of folk dancing in bunches,   15

Of tart wine spilt on home-made benches,

Where hears—one drawn ~~apa~~ aside—a secret will

Restore the dead, but ~~coming~~ comes then to a wall

Outside on frozen soil lie armies killed

Who seem familiar but they are cold.   20

Now the most solid wish he tries to keep

His hands show through. He never will look up

Now, F/feeling ~~his~~ good. On him misfortune falls

             be

More than enough. Better to ~~lie with~~ f where fools

And wise are unmarked, where none stand or sit,   25

~~At cover, too deep for shafts,~~ t/The out-of-sight, too deep for shafts.

                    Harborne August 1928.

The spring unsettles sleeping partnerships:
Foundries impose ~~upon~~ their ~~processes~~ process, and shops
Open a further wing   on credit till
The winter. The summer boys grow tall
With running races on the wetted sand;
War is declared there, here a treaty signed;
Here a scream breaks up like a band, ten troops
Deploy like birds. But coming fatter times
Brandish. The guns which ran in oil for weeks
By ~~week~~ week, needing no looks, now idle not works.
Those manors mortgaged twice to pay for love
Go to another.

        O how shall man live,
His thought born, child of one farcical night
To find him old. The always treatise but not
By choice; he dreams of folk dancing in breeches,
Of tart wine spilt on homemade benches,
Where leans - one dream often aside - a secret will
Restore the dead, but ~~coming~~ comes then to a wall
Outside an frozen soil the armies killed
Who seem familiar but they are cold.
Now the most solid wish he tries to keep
His hands slue through. He never will look up,
Now, feeling ~~him~~ good. On him misfortune falls
More than enough. Better to ~~be~~ ~~instead~~ these fools
For wise an unmarked, where none stand or sit,
~~through, too~~ for shafts, the out - of - sight, too deep for shafts.

           Harlem August 1929.

No, not from this life, not from this life is any
Is any to keep; sleep, day, and play would not help there,
Dangerous to new ghost; new ghost learns from many,
Learns from old termers what death is, where.

Who's jealous of his latest company,   5
Or kept back stammering at the word death,
Scared as by summer lightning, now that he,
Life's painful romping over, is out of breath?

Receive one, Easter, who comes to death from life
Grateful as ever girl looks from ship rails,[1]   [10]
Rescued in Africa, returns a wife
To his ancestral property in Wales.

Tapscott[2] Sept 1928.

Who's jealous of his latest company
From one day to the next final to us.
A changed one?/; would use sorrow to deny
Sorrow, to replace death? Sorry/ow is sleeping thus

No, not from this life, not from this life is any   5
F To keep; sleep day and play would not help there
Dangerous to new ghost; new ghost learns from many
Learns from old termers what death is, where?

Revised Dec 1928 Berlin

No, not from this life, not from this life is any
Treasury to keep; sleep, day, and play would not help there,
Dangerous to new ghost; new ghost learns from many,
Learns from old teachers what death is, where.

Whose jealous of his latest company,
Or keeps back stammering at the word Death,
Scared as by summer lightning, now that he,
Child, painful wondering one, is out of health?

Receive me, Greita, who came to Death from life
Grateful to ever quit looks from strife, vails,
Rescued in Africa returns a wife
In his ancestral property in wales.

Taliscott   Sept 1925.

Whose jealous of his latest company
From one day to the next final to us.
A changed me? would use sorrow to deny
Sorrow, to replace Death? Sorrow is sleeping, thus

No, not from this life, not from this life is any
To keep; sleep Day and play would not help there
Dangerous to new ghost; new ghost learns from many
Learns from old teachers what death is, where?

Revised Dec 1925   Redrv

Can speak of trouble, pressure on ~~man~~ men

~~Brought forward into light~~ Born all the time, brought forward into light

For warm dark moan.

Though ~~But~~ heart

~~But heart,~~ ~~Heart~~ fears all ~~that~~ heart cries for, rebuffs with mortal beat

Sky fall, the legs sucked under, adders bite: 5

That prize held out of reach,

Guides the unwilling tread

The asking breath

Till on attended bed

Or in untracked dishonour comes to each   10

His natural death.

We pass our days

           to   e

Speak, man ~~with~~ mán, easy, learning to point

To jump before ladies, to show our scars.

But no   15

~~These faces~~ We were mistaken, these faces are ~~ou~~ not ours

~~W~~ They smile no more when we smile back;

Eyes, ears, mouth, nostrils, bring

News of revolt, inadequate counsel to

An infirm king.   20

O watcher in the dark, you wake   ~~Berlin. October~~ 1928.

Our dream of waking; we feel

Your finger on the flesh that has been skinned

By your bright morning we

See clear what we were doing, that we were vile.   25

           sudden hand

Your ~~fire and wind~~

Shall ~~Can~~ humble great

                       which

Pride, break it, wear down to stumps, old systems ~~that w~~ await

The last transgression of the sea.   Berlin October 1928

Can speak of trouble, pressure on men men
Brought forward into light Burn all the time, brought forward into light
For warm dark moan.
Though that heart
Batchrist, heart fears all that heart cries for, rebuffs with mortal beat
Sky fall, the legs sucked under, arrers life:
That fruit held out of reach,
    Guide the unwilling tread
    The asking breath
    Till an attendes bed
     Or in untracked distances comes to each
    Its natural death.

We pass our days
Speak, man with mean, easy, learning to point
To print before ladies, to show our scars.
    But us
    Them faces We were mistaken, these faces are or not ours
    the They smile no more when we smile back;
     Eyes, ears, mouth nostrils, being
     News of revolt, inadequate armed to
      for no firm king.

O Watcher in the dark, you wake   Berlin October 1928.
On dream of waking; we feel
Your finger on the flesh that has been skinned
By your bright morning we
See clear what we were doing, that we were vile.
                 sudden hand
Your fire and wind
Shall can handle great
        Rinse, break it, wear down to sleep, old system that we want
                      which
        The last transgression of the sea.   Berlin October 1928

There is the city
Lighted and clean once, pleasure for builders
But I
Letting to cheaper tenants, have made a slum
Houses at which the passer shakes his fist
Remembering evil.
Pride and indifference have shared into me, and I
Have kissed them in the dark, for mind has dark,
Shades commemorations, midnight accidents
In streets where heirs may die.

But love sent east for peace
From tunnels under those
Bursts now to pass
On trestles over meaner quarters
A noise and flashing glass.

Eels morning streaming down
Louis from the sewers.
Novice withdrawn by doubting flinch
Nor joined to any by beliefs from change
Refreshes sees all
She triggers at least
She hoffens steady feed, the frothing leak.

                              Berlin   Nov 1928.

There is the city
Lighted and clean once, pleasure for builders
But I
Letting to cheaper tenants, have made a slum
Houses at which the passer shakes his fist   5
Remembering evil.
Pride and indifference have shared with me, and I
Have kissed them in the dark, for mind has dark,
Shaded commemorations, midnight accidents
In streets where heirs may dine.   10

But love sent east for peace
From tunnels under those
Bursts now to pass
On trestles over meaner quarters
A noise and flashing glass.   15

Feels morning streaming down
Wind from the snows.
Nowise withdrawn by doubting flinch
Nor joined to any by belief's firm flange
Refreshed sees all   20
The tugged-at teat
The hopper's steady feed, the frothing leat.

                    Berlin Nov 1928.

       lived
If I ~~were living~~ in the country and you lived in the town
You would send books and the news
I, a brace of game or a hamper of fruit in season

If you were rich and I were wise
           new
You would ~~buy me clothes~~ offer me food and drink   5
And I would tell you a word meaning the best.

Same/time sharers of the same house
We know not the builder nor the name of his son
              them
Now cannot ~~pa~~ mean to ~~past~~ — boy's voice among dishonoured portraits
To dock-side barmaid speaking   10
Sorry through wires, pretended speech.

Armies pursuit, rebellion and eclipse
Escaping in a cart
After all journeys.
    stay
We ~~rest~~ and are not known.   15

Sharers of the same house
Attendants on the same machine
Of few words, in silence understan/ood.

                  Berlin
                    Nov 1928.

If I ~~were living~~ [lives] in the country and you lived in the town
You would send books and the news
I, a hare of game or a hamper of fruit in season

If you were rich and I were wise
You would ~~buy me clothes~~ [new] offer me food or drink
And I, would tell you a word meaning the best.

Sometime sharers of the same house
We know not the builder nor the name of his son
Nor cannot ~~to meant~~ [then] flesh – boys voice any Dishonored patriots
To dock-side barmaid speaking
Sorry through wires, pretended speech.

Armies pursuit, rebellion and eclipse
Escaping in a cart
After all journeys.
We ~~rest~~ [stay] and are not known,

Sharers of the same house
Attendants on the same machine
Of few words, in silence understood.

Berlin
Nov 1928

Always the following wind of history
Of others' wisdom makes a buoyant air
Till we come suddenly on pockets where
Is nothing loud but us, where voices seem
Abrupt, untrained, comforting with no lie
Our father's started. They taught us war,
To scamper after darlings, to climb hills,
To emigrate from weakness, find ourselves
The easy conquerors of empty bays;
But never told us this, left each to learn,
Hear something of that soon arriving day
When to gaze longer and delighted on
A lesser or district be impossible.
Could I have been some simpleton that lived
Before disaster sent his runners here,
Longer than walking, walking have too much to bear,
Yes minerals were best. ~~I saw~~ could I but see
A green field longer thick
With smoking alkali, this lovely world
~~~~ sterile as the moons.

Always the following wind of history
Of others' wisdom makes a buoyant air
Till we come suddenly on pockets where
Is nothing loud but us, where voices seem
Abrupt, untrained, competing with no lie   5
Our fathers shouted. They taught us war,
To scamper after darlings, to climb hills,
To emigrate from weakness, find ourselves
The easy conquerors of empty bays,/:
But never told us this, left each to learn,   10
Hear something of that soon arriving day
When to gaze longer and delighted on
A face or district be impossible.
Could I have been some simpleton that lived
Before disaster sent his runners here,   15
Younger than worms, worms have too much to bear.
Yes mineral were best. ~~Or that I saw~~ could I but see
A green field layered thick
With smoking alkali,[1] this lively world
~~As~~ sterile as ~~the~~ moon/s.   20

Because I'm come, it does not mean to hold
An anniversary, think illness healed,
As to renew the lease, consider costs
Of derelict ironworks on deserted coasts.
Nothing was any use; therefore I went   5
Hearing you call for what you did not want.
I lay with you. You made that an excuse
For playing with yourself, but homesick because
Your mother told you that's what flowers did,¹   15
And thought you lived since you were bored not dead,   [10]
And could not stop. ~~I tried then to demand~~ ~~Then~~/So I was cold to make

                quickly
~~Every proud habit which you thought as ea mind~~ No difference but you were ~~basely~~ meek
~~To show i~~ Altered for safety. I tried then to demand
All those proud habits which you called as mind   20
To show ~~it~~ you it was extra, but instead   [15]
You overworked yourself, misunderstood,
Adored me for the chance. Lastly I thought
That we would play at royalty for that
~~W~~ Is easiest. ~~You were in love~~   [20]
~~And thought me grand, real acting the real life,~~
~~but would not act yourself~~ for you had nerves   25
And feared performances as some fear knives.
Love was not love for you but episodes
Traffic in memoirs, views from different sides.
             ~~must~~ a
You thought oaths of comparison ~~would~~ ~~bind~~/bond   [25]
And when you had your orders to disband   10
Refused to   remained
~~You would not~~ listen, but ~~stayed~~ in woods
Poorly concealed your profits under wads.
Now I shall go. ~~now.~~ No you, if you come
Will not enjoy yourself for where I am   [30]
All talking is forbidden.²   Berlin Nov 1928

[PAGE 143]

Because I'm come, it does not mean to hold
An anniversary, think illness healed,
Or to renew the lease, consider costs
Of derelict ironworks on deserted coasts.
Nothing was any use; therefore I went
Hearing you call for what you did not want.

I lay with you. You made that an excuse
For playing with yourself, but homesick because
Your mother told you that's what flowers did,
And thought you lived since you were bored not dead,
And could not stop. ~~I tried then to demand~~ ~~And I was~~ old to make
~~very fixed habit which you thought as errand~~ No difference but you were barely ~~wash~~ quickly made
~~To show it~~ Altered for safety. I tried then to demand
All those fixed habits which you called as mind
To show ~~them~~ you it was extra, but instead
You overworked yourself, misunderstood,
Adored me for the chance. Lastly I thought
That we would play at royalty for that
Is Is easiest. ~~You were in love~~
~~Not thought on grant, real acting~~ the real life,
But would not ~~act yourself~~ for you had never
Any fewer performances as some fear knives.

Love was not love for you but episodes
Traffic in memories, views from different sides.
You thought ~~oaths~~ of comparison ~~would~~ such a ~~boys~~
And when you had your orders to disband
You ~~would not~~ Refuse to listen, but ~~stays~~ remained in woods
Poorly concealed your profits under words.
Now I shall go, ~~you~~. No you, if you come
Will not enjoy yourself for where I am
All talking is forbidden.

                                        Berlin Nov 1928

Yesterday we sat at table together

Tonight side by side at enemies face to face meeting

To day we take our leave, time [for] of departure.

The badger moves knows in ~~Gunter's~~ Gunter's wood

The salmon feeds in ~~the~~ tributaries of the lake ~~stream~~.

Give me your knife. Take mine. By these

let my remember each other.

There are two chances but man of one

   Parting for ever, not leaving the other

   Though he need help.

                              Berlin.   Dec 1928

Yesterday we sat at table together
Fought side by side at enemies' face to face meeting
Today we take our leave, time ~~fo~~/of departure.
                 ~~H[?]~~   Quester's
The badger ~~in a~~ burrows in ~~Hampstead~~ wood
                             tributaries of the Kell
The salmon feeds in ~~riv~~ the ~~river stream near Haykell~~.   5

Give me your knife. Take mine. By these
We may remember each other.
There are two chances but more of one
Parting for ever, not hearing the other
Though he need help.   10

            Berlin. Dec 1928

Bo

In these days during the migrations, days
Freshening with rain reported in the mountains
By loss of memory we*t* are reborn
For memory is death, by taking leave
Parting in anger and glad to go   5
Where we are still unwelcome: and ~w~/if we count
What dead the tides wash in, only to make
Notches for enemies. On northern ridges,
Where flags fly, seen and lost, denying rumours
We baffle proof, speakers of a strange tongue.   10

Po

~After~ Past victor~ies~/y is honour, to accept
        An island governorship, back to estates
        Explored as child, coming at last to love
        Lost publicly, found secretly again
        In private flats, admitted to a sign,/.   5
        And~,~ understanding sorrow~,~ know/s no more,
        Sit[s] waiting for the lamp, far from those hills
        Where rifts open unfenced, mark of a fall
        And flakes fall softly softly burying
        Deeper and deeper down, her loving son   10

                                    Berlin
                                    Dec 1928.

[PAGE 145: a, b]

No

In those days, during the migrations, Days
Freshening with rain reported in the mountains
By loss of memory we are reborn
For memory is death, by taking leave
Parting in anger and glad to go
Where we are still unwelcome: and if we count
What dead the tides wash in, only to make
Notches for enemies. On northern reefs,
Where flags fly, seen and lost, Denying rumours
Or baffle proof, sketches of a strange tongue.

No

~~After~~ Nor victories is known, to accept
An island queenship, back to solitude
Exposed as child, coming at last to love
Lost publicly, find secretly again
In private flats, admitted to a sign,
And, understanding sorrow, know no more,
Sit waiting for the lamp, far from those hills
Where rifts often unfences, marked a fall
And flakes fall softly softly burying
Deeper and deeper down, her loving son

Berlin
Dec 1928.

We made all possible preparations
Drew up a list of firms
Constantly revised our calculations
And allotted the farms.

Issued all the orders expedient   5
In this kind of case
Most as was expected were obedient
Though there were murmurs of course

Chiefly against our exercising   10
Our old right to abuse
Even some sort of attempt at rising
But these were mere boys

For never serious misgiving
Occurred to anyone
Since there could be no question of living   15
If we did not win.

.   .   .   .

The generally accepted view teaches
That there was no excuse
Though in the light of recent researches
Many would find the cause   20

In a not uncommon form of terror
Others still more astute
Point to possibilities of error
At the very start

[cont. on p 153]

We made all possible preparations
Drew up a list of firms
Constantly revised our calculations
And allotted the farms.

Issued all the orders expedient
In this kind of case
Most were satisfied when disbursed
Though there were murmurs of course

Chiefly against our exercising
Our old right to abuse
Even some sort of attempt at rising
But these were mere boys

For never serious misgiving
Occurred to anyone
Since there could be no question of living
If we did not win.

- - - - - - - - -

The generally accepted view teaches
That there was no excuse
Though in the light of recent researches
Many would find the cause

In a not uncommon form of terror
Others still more astute
Point to foreknowledge of error
At the very start

As for ourselves there is left remaining

Our honour at least

And a reasonable chance of retaining

Our faculties to the last.

Berlin Dec 1928.

As for ourselves there is left remaining
Our honour at least
And a reasonable chance of retaining
Our faculties to the last.

Berlin   Dec 1928.

Again in conversations
Speaking of fear
And throwing off reserve
The voice is nearer
But no clearer   5
Than first love
Than peace-time occupations.

For every news
Means pairing off in twos and twos
Another I, another You   10
Each knowing what to do
But of no use.

Never stronger
But younger and younger
Saying goodbye but coming back, for fear   15
Is over there
And the centre of anger
Is out of danger.

Berlin.

Jan. 1929.

Again in conversations
Speaking of fear
And throwing off reserve
The voice is nearer
But no clearer
Than first love
Than boys-time inspiration.

For every news
Means pairing off in twos and twos
Another I, another You
Each knowing what to do
But of no use.

Never stronger
But younger and younger
Saying goodbye but coming back, for fear
Is over there
For the centre of anger
Is out of danger.

Berlin.
Jan. 1929.

Head asleep
Falling forward[1]
Must stop and go backward
Must keep, hard to keep
Its old importance, its chief position   5

Early relaxation
And trustful features
Expect no signs
Forgetting virtues
Still advertised on local lines.   10
Heros/es have fallen into vats and stewed
But men drink up their beer unknowing
Drink deep
And hurried sleep
For other going   15
Were to intrude.

But trusted here
Choosing to tell
A chosen listener
Slapstick adventures, views from holidays   20
Receive due praise
Praise giving and taking
Before waking
And reproachful morning
All is well   25
Each act has place
Each word has number
And praise takes breath
Before death
For death is a case   Berlin. Jan. 1929   30
With no examples to remember.

Head asleep
Falling forward
Must stop and go backward
Must keep, hard to keep
Its old importance, its chief position

Early relaxation
Of trustful features
Expect no signs
Forgetting virtues
Still advertised on local lines.
Heroes have fallen into vats and stews
But men drink up their beer unknowing
Drink deep
Of hurried sleep
For others going
Soon to intrude.

But trusted here
Choosing to tell
A chosen listener.
Slapstick adventures, views from holidays
Receive due praise
Praise giving and taking,
Before waking
Of reproachful morning
All is well
Each act has place
Each word has number
Of praise takes breath
Before death
For death is a case
With no examples to remember.

Berlin. Jan. 49

She has been here for three months looking for employment
When she buys a pair of stockings she leaves them in the bus

In the hotel the married Englishman
With the chauffeur on his knee
Said "I hear the parties in Cambridge
Are hot stuff nowadays

He was a housemaster and a bachelor
But refused to keep dogs
So he is dying of cancer

The mother had wanted
To be a missionary in Africa
So the son's novel
Must be published in Paris

He is a psychologist
But won't lend his handkerchief

The friends of the town nurse
She always falling ill

Smith likes butcher boys
And's therefore a conservative
Jones is a socialist
Because he likes duchesses
Jones can't have dud duchesses
So Smith's nicer

She has been here for three months looking for employment
When she buys a pair of stockings she leaves them in the bus

In the local the married Englishman
With the chauffeur on his knee
Said "I hear the parties in Cambridge
Are hot stuff nowadays"

He was a housemaster and a bachelor
But refused to keep dogs
So he is dying of cancer

The mother had wanted
To be a missionary in Africa
So the son's novel
Must be published in Paris

He is a psychologist
But won't lend his handkerchief

The friends of the born nurse
Are always falling ill

Smith likes butcher boys
Smith is therefore a conservative
Jones is a socialist
Because he likes duchesses
Jones can't have ~~dul~~ duchesses
So Smith is nicer

5

From scars where kestrels[1] hover
The leader looking over
Into the happy valley
Orchard and curving river
May turn away to see   5
The slow fastidious line
That disciplines the fell[2]
Hear curlews creaking call
From angles unforeseen
The drumming of a snipe   10
Surprise where driven sleet
Has/d scalded to the bone
And streams are acid yet
To an unaccustomed lip:[3]
The tall unwounded leader   15
Of doomed companions, all
Whose voices in the rock
Are now perpetual
Fighters for no one's sake
Who died beyond the border   20

The heroes are buried who
Did not believe in death
And bravery is now
Not in the dying breath
But resisting the temptations   25
To sky-line operations.

Yet glory is not new
The summer visitors
Still come from far and wide

[cont. on p 165]

From scars where kestrels hover
The leader looking over
Into the happy valley
Orchard and curving river
May turn away to see
The slow fastidious line
That disciplines the field
(Hear curlews creating calm)
Can angles unforeseen
The drumming of a snipe
Surprise where driven sheet
Has scalded to the bone
Pur streams are acid yet
To an unaccustomed lip:
The tale unwanted leader
Of doomed companions, all
Whose voices in the rock
Are now perpetual
Fighters, for no man's sake
Who died beyond the border

The heroes are buried who
Did not believe in death
And haven to now
Not in the dying heather
Nor resisting the temptation
To skyline operations.

Yet glory is not new
The summer visiting
Still come for far and wide

Choosing their spots to view   30
The prize competitors
Each thinking that he will
Find heroes in the wood
Far from the capital

Where lights and wine are set   35
For supper by the lake
But leaders must migrate
"Leave for Cape Wrath[4] to-night
Shall not arrive this week
Nor any week. Writing"   40
And the host after waiting
Must quench the lamps and pass
Alive into the house.

                    Berlin. Jan 1929.

choosing their spots to view
The future competitors
Each the aching that he will
Find haven in the wood
Far from the capitol

Where lights and wine are set
For supper by the lake
But leaders must migrate
"Leave for Cafe Wrath tonight
Shall not arrive this week
Nor any week. Writing"
And the heart often wanting
But quench the lamps and pass
Alive into the house.

Berlin. Jan 1929.

①

Under boughs between our tentative endearments, how should we hear
But with flushing pleasure drums, distant over difficult country,
      Events not actual
      In Time's unlenient will?

Which we shall not avoid, though at a station's chance delay   5
Lines branch to peace, iron up valleys to a hidden village,[1]
      For we have friends to catch
      And none leave coach:

                          but
Sharers of our own day, thought smiling of, ~~and~~ nothing known
What industries decline, what chances are of revolution,   10
      What murders flash
      Under composed flesh.

Knowledge no need to us whose wrists enjoy the chafing leash,
Can plunder high nests; who sheer off from old like gull from granite,
      From their mind's constant sniffling   15
      Their blood's dulled shuffling.

Who ~~These~~, feebling, still have time to wonder at the well-shaped heads
Conforming every day more closely to the best in albums,
      Fathers in sons may track
      Their voices' trick.   20

Earth unencumbered but far richer is by these sunk in,
These generations huddled underground may freshen morning
      Their bodies changed to gas
      Filtered through grass.

[cont. on p 171]

Under boughs between our tentative endearments, how should we hear
But with flushing pleasure drums, distant over difficult country,
Events not actual
In Time's unlenient will?

Which we shall not avoid, though at a station's chance delay
Lines branch to peace, turn up valleys to a hidden village,
For we have friends to catch
And none leave coach:

Shame of one arm day, thought smiling of, but and nothing known
What industries decline, what chances are of revolution,
What murders flash
Under composed flesh.

Knowledge no need to us whose wrists enjoy the chafing leash,
Can plunder high nests; who sheer off from old like quill from granite,
From their minds constant sniffling
Their mood's dulled chaffing.

Who free, fretting, still have time to wonder at the well-shaped heads
Conforming every day more closely to the best in albums.
Fathers in sons may track
Their voices track.

Youth unencumbered but far richer is by these sunk in,
Dear generations huddles underground may freshen meaning
Their bodies changed to gas
Filtered through grass.

But their ancestral curse, jumbled perhaps and put away,   [25]
Baffled for years, at last in one repeats its potent pattern
        And blows fall more than once
        Although he wince,

          a
Though to ~~the~~ moorland market town retired for work or love,   25
May creep to sumps, pile up against the door, crouching in cases,   [30]
        This anger falling,
        Opens, empties that filling.

Let each one share our pity, hard to withhold and hard to bear
None knows of the next day if it be less or more, the sorrow,   30
        Escaping cannot try,   [35]
        Must wait though it destroy.

                  Berlin. March 1929.

But their ancestral curse, jumbled perhaps and put away,
Baulked for years, at last in one repeats its potent pattern
Two blows fall more than once
Although he wince,

Though to the moorland market town returns for work or love,
They creep to shrubs, pile up against the door, crouching in caves,
This anger falling,
Blows, empties that filling.

Let each one share our pity, hard to withhold and hard to bear
None knows of the next day if it be less or more, the sorrow,
Escaping cannot try,
But wait though it destroy.

                                        Berlin. March 1929.

Put your legs on the table
And don't go near the wall
Your ~~father's~~ master's ~~out~~ at elbow
Your ~~mother~~ mistress cries in the hall.

Put your legs on the table

And don't go near the wall
    ~~father's~~ master's
Your ~~master's~~ out at elbow
    ~~mother~~ mistress
Your ~~mistress~~ cries in the hall.

Love by ambition
Of definition
Suffers partition
And cannot go
f/From yes to no: 5
For no is not love, no is no,
The shutting of a door
A̶/The tightening jaw
A conscious sorrow:
And saying yes   10
Turns love into success
Views from the rail[1]
Of land and happiness.
Assured of all
The sofas creak   15
And were this all, love were
But cheek to cheek
And dear to dear.

Voices explain
Love's pleasure and love's pain   20
Still tap the knee
And cannot disagree
Hushed for aggression
Of full confession
L̶i̶k̶e̶ ̶t̶o̶ Likeness to likeness   25
Of each old weakness
Love is not there
Love has moved to another chair

[cont. on p 175]

Love by ambition
Of definition
Suffers partition
And cannot go
From yes to no:
For no is not love, no is no,
The shutting of a door
The tightening jaw,
A conscious sorrow:
And saying yes
Turns love into success
View from the vail
Of lands and happiness.
Assured of all
The sofas creak
And were this all, love were
But cheek to cheek
And dear to dear.

Voices as plain
Loves pleasure and love's pain
Still tell the know
And cannot disagree
Hushes for a question
Of false confession
~~Like to~~ listen to listeners
Of each old weakness
Love is not there
Love has moved to another chair

Aware already
Of who stands next   30
And is not vexed
And is not giddy
Leaves the north in place
With a good grace²
And would not gather   35
Another to another,
Designs his own unhappiness
Foretells his own death and is faithless.

                              Berlin. March 1929

Aware already
Of who stands next
This is not verse
This is not giddy
Leaves the world in place
With a good grace
This would not gather
Brother to another,
Designs his own unhappiness
But tells his own death and is faithless.

Berlin. March 1929

Before this loved one
Was that one and that one
A family
And history
And ghost's[1] adversity   5
Whose pleasing name
Was neighbourly shame.
Before this last one
Was much to be done
Frontiers to cross   10
As clothes grew worse
And coins to pass
In a cheaper house
Before this last one
Before this loved one.   15

Face that the sun
Is supple, on
May stir but, here
Is no new, year.
The gratitude for gifts is less   20
Than the old loss,
Touching is shaking hands
Our mortgaged lands
And smiling of
This gracious greeting   25
'good day, good luck'
Is no real meeting
But remembered look
A backward love.[2]

                    Berlin. March 1929

Before this loved me   .
Was that one and that one
A family
And history
And ghosts' adversity
Whose pleasing name
Was neighbourly shame.
Before this last one
Was much to be done
Frontiers to cross
To clothes grew worse
And coming to pass
In a cheaper house
Before this last one
Before this loved me.

For that the sun
Is supple, or
May stir but here
Is no new year.
The gratitude for gifts is less
Than the old loss,
Touching to shaking hands
On mortgaged lands
And smiling of
This gracious greeting
'good day, good luck'
Is no real meeting
But remembered look
A backward love.

Berlin. March 1929

Watch any day his nonchalant pauses; see
His dextrous handling of a wrap ~~as~~ he ^as^
Steps after into cars, the beggar's envy.

"There is the free one" many say, but err;
He is not that returning conqueror   5
Nor ever the poles' circumnavigator.

But poised between shocking falls, on razor edge
Has taught himself this balancing subterfuge
Of the accosting profile, the erect carriage.

The song, the varied motions of the blood   10
Would drown the warning from the iron wood,[1]
Would cancel the inertia of the buried.

Travelling by ~~da~~ daylight on from place to place
The longest way to the intrinsic peace
With love's fidelity and with love's weakness.   15

Berlin. March 1929.

Watch any day his nonchalant pauses; see
His dextrous handling of a map as he
Steps after into cars, the beggar's envy.

"There is the free one" many say, but err;
He is not that returning conqueror
Nor ever the poles' circumnavigator.

But poised between shocking falls, on razor edge
Has taught himself this balancing subterfuge
Of the accosting profile, the erect carriage.

To say, the varied actions of the blood
Would dam the warning from the icu wood,
Would cancel the initia of the buried.

Travelling by daylight on from place to place
The longest way to the intrinsic peace
With his fidelity and into his weakness.

Berlin. March 1929.

l
ter way
xs
ent

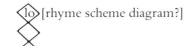[rhyme scheme diagram?]

ry

—

ley

ment
d

l

A J A

W H A's scale of sins—least to most
    GLUTTONY
    LUST
    SLOTH
    ANGER
    AVARICE
    EN¥/VY
    PRIDE

a g a

WHA's scale of sins- least to most

GLUTTONY
LUST
SLOTH
ANGER
AVARICE
ENVY
PRIDE

Editor's Notes

THE NOTEBOOK is an "Account Book" manufactured by H. P. Pope, Ltd, Birmingham. The cover is moiré fine-rib cloth, deep purplish blue, with a dotted-line cloth, deep purplish blue spine. The paper is yellowish white, laid, unwatermarked with lines (33 to a page). In its original state the notebook comprised six folio gatherings, with sixteen leaves to a gathering. The first and last pages were pasted down, leaving 190 pages. Auden removed fifty-five leaves, so that the notebook as it now exists comprises eighty pages, twenty of which are blank. Where noted below, some of the stubs of removed pages have a few fragments of writing.

Collation: 2°. 32 x 20 cm. [A–F¹⁶].

Pagination (italicized numbers indicate missing pages): 96 leaves; [1 pasted down, 2, *3–4*, *5–8*, *9–32*, 33–34, *35–36*, 37–46, *47–50*, 51–54, *55–56*, 57–60, *61–64*, 65–70, *71–88*, 89–90, *91* stub, *92*, 93–96, *97–98*, *99* stub, *100*, 101–06, *107–16*, 117–20, *121–22*, 123–24, *125–34*, *135* stub, *136–40*, 141–46, *147–50*, 151–58, *159–62*, 163–66, *167–68*, 169–76, *177–80*, 181–84, *185–87*, *188* stub, *189–90*, 191, 192 pasted down]. Pages 34, 38, 70, 94, 102, 104, 106, 118, 120, 146, 152, 154, 156, 164, 166, 170, 174, 176, 182, and 184 are blank.

The number in square brackets ([ ]) on the transcription pages is the original page number according to the above pagination (the cataloguer's numbers pencilled on the top right of the notebook's recto pages may be ignored).

Certain editorial notations have been added to the transcription. Pencilled words and marks are printed in red; those in ink, in black. The arrow (←) following a line of verse or a word points out an annotation by Auden on the opposite page; the following marks and abbreviations are also used:

$p^{/i}$	pencilled word or line written over with ink (in one case this is reversed)—if only a deletion line is so rewritten (and the words are in ink alone, as is usually the case), the superscript note follows the line, which has been extended slightly beyond the words crossed out
rev.	revision/revised
word/word or suffix (e.g., on/upon)	original word (or portion of word)/revision (in the example, Auden first wrote "on" and revised it to "upon").

The deletion marks on the transcription indicate the probable start and end of Auden's intended deletion in the text (these do not always duplicate the exact position of the manuscript marks).

The line numbers with the transcription refer to the final version of a poem on the notebook page(s). The line numbers within square brackets refer to the probable numbering of an earlier stage of the poem before revision, as it appears in the notebook.

A few slips of the pen have been silently corrected in the transcription (corrections are indicated in the notes) and obvious closing quotation marks or apostrophes added for clarity even if not visible in the manuscript. Note that Auden uses both single and double quotation marks. In the transcription, editorial conjectures are followed by a question mark or included within square brackets. Editorial apparatus has been kept as simple as possible to facilitate the reading of the poems in their various stages.

In the notes which follow, these abbreviations are used to direct the reader to the publication of any given poem in Auden's principal works:

P28	*Poems* (S. H. S[pender] 1928)
P30	*Poems* (Faber 1930)
P34	*Poems* (Random House 1934)
SP	*Selected Poems* (Faber 1938)
SoP	*Some Poems* (Faber 1940)
CP	*The Collected Poetry of W. H. Auden* (Random House 1945)
CSP	*Collected Shorter Poems, 1930–1944* (Faber 1950)
SP2	*W. H. Auden: A Selection by the Author* (Penguin 1958)
CSP2	*Collected Shorter Poems, 1927–1957* (Faber 1966)
SP3	*Selected Poems* (Faber 1968)
CLP	*Collected Longer Poems* (Faber 1968)
EA	*The English Auden* (Faber 1977)
SP4	*Selected Poems* (Random House 1979)
CP2	*Collected Poems* (The Franklin Library 1980).

It is important to note that the notebook and transcription contain the accurate text of most of the poems printed in Auden's first book (*P28*), which had many misprints, and somewhat different, usually earlier, texts from the final versions of Auden's early poems printed in *EA*.

Acknowledgments

This book was produced with much help from my former colleagues at The New York Public Library, the designer Marilan Lund and the poet William Leo Coakley. At all stages of the project, Professor Edward Mendelson, Literary Executor of the Auden Estate, generously gave of his advice and of his knowledge of Auden's work and life.

January 1989

P.T.L.

Notes to the Transcription

1   Auden was interested in Freudian theories
from an early age. His two major treatments of
Freud are: "Psychology and Art To-day" (*EA*,
332), in which he explores Freud's "attitude to
life and living relationships . . . and its impor-
tance to creative art," and "In Memory of Sig-
mund Freud," the famous elegy of November
1939. Auden's debt to Freud should not be over-
stressed. As Edward Mendelson writes in *Early
Auden* (New York: Viking Press 1981) 41, "the
detailed psychological theory in Auden's poems
derived less from Freud himself than from such
variously heterodox psychologists as Trigant
Burrow, Georg Groddeck, Eugen Bleuler, and
William McDougall. In his interpretations of art-
ists, Auden wrote in *Letter to Lord Byron*, 'Freud's
not quite O.K.'"

2   Trigant Burrow (1875–1950), "phylobiolo-
gist" and psychiatrist. One of the earliest Freud-
ians in the United States, Burrow began his
study of relationships in 1918 and in 1927 pub-
lished *The Social Basis of Consciousness*, in which
he reported on his new method of group analy-
sis. Through a method of collective analysis—
"phyloanalysis"—he believed that neurosis could
be abolished. Burrow emphasized the total phys-
ical and mental reaction of not only the holistic
individual but the entire human race.

3   Bronislaw Malinowski (1884–1942), Polish
anthropologist. Malinowski joined the Mond ex-
pedition to Melanesia in 1914 and spent the next
six years studying primitive societies. A brilliant
field-worker and able theorist, he was soon rec-
ognized as one of the leading anthropologists of
his day. His publications include: *The Family
among the Australian Aborigines* (1913); *Crime and
Custom in Savage Society* (1926); *Sex and Repres-
sion in Savage Society* (1927), and *The Sexual Life
of Savages in N.W. Melanesia* (1929). In "Heavy
Date" (*CP*, 105) Auden writes:

> Malinowski, Rivers,
> Benedict and others
> Show how common culture
>   Shapes the separate lives:
> Matrilineal races
> Kill their mothers' brothers
> In their dreams and turn their
>   Sisters into wives.

4   Kurt Koffka (1886–1941), psychologist.
Koffka, along with Wolfgang Köhler and Max
Wertheimer, is credited with the development of
Gestalt theory. Although not the most original
of the trio, Koffka became their most influential
spokesman. His monumental work, *Principles of
Gestalt Psychology*, was published in 1935.

5   The price of the notebook in a shopkeeper's
hand.

1   (Opposite line 2 of "The sprinkler on the
lawn," p [7a].) St Edmunds. In *W. H. Auden: A
Biography* (Boston: Houghton Mifflin 1981)
Humphrey Carpenter paints an excellent picture
of life at St Edmund's School at Hindhead in
Surrey, "a preparatory establishment of some
fifty boys" (16) where Auden was sent in the
autumn of 1915. His brother John was also at St
Edmund's. In "The Prolific and the Devourer"
(*EA*, 398) Auden writes:

> My political education began at the age of
> seven when I was sent to a boarding school
> [St Edmund's]. Every English boy of the
> middle class spends five years as a member
> of a primitive tribe ruled by benevolent or
> malignant demons, and then another five
> years as a citizen of a totalitarian state.
>
> For the first time I came in contact with
> adults outside the family circle and found
> them to be hairy monsters with terrifying
> voices and eccentric habits, completely irra-
> tional in their bouts of rage and good-
> humour, and, it seemed, with absolute
> power of life and death.

[PAGE 6, continued]

2   "Amoeba in the running water"—*P28*, I(g);
EA, 438.

In *The Poetry of W. H. Auden* (New York:
Oxford University Press 1963) 29, Monroe K.
Spears conjectures that the model for this poem
is "Walter de la Mare, in such poems as 'Song of
the Mad Prince'":

> Who said, 'Peacock Pie'?
>   The old King to the sparrow:
> Who said, 'Crops are ripe'?
>   Rust to the harrow:
> Who said, 'Where sleeps she now?
>   Where rests she now her head,
> Bathed in eve's loveliness'?—
>   That's what I said

(from "The Song of the Mad Prince" in *A Choice
of de la Mare's Verse* Selected with an Introduction
by W. H. Auden [London: Faber 1963] 127).

3   (Opposite line 4 of "The Megalopsych, says
Aristotle," p [7c].) Wilfred Owen (1893–1918),
poet. Owen enlisted in the First World War, but
was invalided in 1917 and sent to a war hos-
pital where he met Siegfried Sassoon, who en-
couraged him to write poetry. Sent back to the
front, he was killed a week before armistice. His
posthumously published *Poems* (1920) were col-
lected by Sassoon. The line quoted by Auden
comes in stanza six of "Insensibility" (*The Poems
of Wilfred Owen* ed Jon Stallworthy [London:
Hogarth Press 1985] 123):

> But cursed are dullards whom no cannon
>   stuns,
> That they should be as stones.
> Wretched are they, and mean
> With paucity that never was simplicity.

[PAGE 7: a–c]

1   John Bicknell Auden (b. 1903), the poet's
brother.

2   "The sprinkler on the lawn"—*P28*, I(a); *EA*,
437.

The deleted roman numeral one is probably
from Auden's numbering of the order of poems
in his first book (this poem does begin the book).

3   "Bones wrenched, weak whimper, lids wrin-
kled, first dazzle known"—*P28*, I(b); *P30*, XIII;
EA, 21.

Line [5]—suffits: perhaps one of the variant spell-
ings of 'soffit' (*OED*), the undersurface of an
arch, used metaphorically in the sense of 'arches'.

4   "The Megalopsych, says Aristotle"—unpub-
lished.

The *OED* makes reference from Megalo-
psychy (an obsolete word, from the Greek, a
noun of quality) to Megalopsychic (a nonce-
word, from the Greek 'great souled'; Magnani-
mous).

[PAGE 8]

The three explanatory notes on this page refer to
a facing page which Auden removed.

1   T. S. Eliot "Whispers of Immortality," lines
1–8 (*Collected Poems 1909–1962* [London: Faber
1963] 55):

> Webster was much possessed by death
> And saw the skull beneath the skin;
> And breathless creatures under ground
> Leaned backward with a lipless grin.
>
> Daffodil bulbs instead of balls
> Stared from the sockets of the eyes!
> He knew that thought clings round dead
>   limbs
> Tightening its lusts and luxuries.

It is probable that the quotation from Eliot refers
to the following lines from "We saw in Spring"
(*P28*, I[c]):

> In Spring we saw
> The bulb pillow
> Raising the skull,
> Thrusting a crocus through clenched teeth.

[PAGE 33]

"No trenchant parting this"—*P28*, III; *P30*,
XXVII; *EA*, 21.

The deleted "1" is probably from a tentative
numbering of the order of poems in Auden's first
book—see fn. 2 to p [7a], above.

1   " 'The diver's brilliant bow' . . . is used in 'As
I walked out one evening'" (Spears, 69):

> Into many a green valley
>   Drifts the appalling snow;
> Time breaks the threaded dances
>   And the diver's brilliant bow.
>   (*CP*, 197)

2   In July 1927, after completing his second year at Oxford, Auden and his father visited Yugoslavia: "The trip was apparently not a success. 'I once went to Yugoslavia with father and wished I was dead,' Auden wrote some years later" (Carpenter, 73).

Line 13—squiny: 'squint', *OED*. This was misread as "squint" in *P28*, corrected in *P30*.

[PAGE 37]

"Who stands, the crux left of the watershed"— *P28*, VI; *P30*, XI; *P34*, 22; *CP*, 175: "The Watershed"; *CSP*, 183; *CSP2*, 22; *SP3*, 8; *EA*, 22; *SP4*, 1; *CP2*, 25.

This is the first poem Auden considered significant enough to be preserved as part of his canon: "it was the first piece that, looking back, he judged to be mature and competent" (Carpenter, 73). In *A Reader's Guide to W. H. Auden* (New York: Farrar, Straus & Giroux 1970) 34, John Fuller notes that in 1926 Auden published a poem in *Oxford Outlook* (VIII 119) entitled "Lead's the Best" with a similar setting. "[In this poem Auden] frees himself from the manner of Eliot by reclaiming from Hardy what he later called Hardy's 'hawk's vision, his way of looking at life from a very great height'" (Mendelson, 33).

1   The Auden family moved into 42 Lordswood Road, Harborne, Birmingham in 1918.

[PAGE 39]

"Suppose they met, the inevitable procedure"— *P28*, IV; *P30*, XXV; *EA*, 22.

1   "Towards the end of the summer vacation of 1927, Auden travelled to the north of Scotland, where, at Carr Bridge near Inverness, he joined a reading party of undergraduates organised by Ernest Jacob, tutor in medieval history at Christ Church" (Carpenter, 73). In *W. H. Auden: A Bibliography* by B. C. Bloomfield and Edward Mendelson (Charlottesville: University of Virginia Press 1972) 246, there is a description of a 7-page manuscript in the University of Texas Library which contains a copy of this poem, with its place of composition as Dalbuich.

Lines 9 and 12—the square brackets are not deletion marks—Auden used the third stanza within parentheses in *P28* and *P30*.

[PAGE 40]

1   (Opposite lines 1–4 of "The crowing of the cock," p [41].) Aurelius Prudentius Clemens *Liber Cathemerinon* II, lines 1–4 (Corpus Christianorum: Series Latina, 126 [Turnholti: Brepols 1966] 7); Sister M. Clement Eagan, tr *The Poems of Prudentius* The Fathers of the Church: A New Translation, 43 [Washington, D.C.: Catholic University of America Press 1962] 8):

> *Hymnus Matutinus*
> Nox et tenebrae et nubila
> confusa mundi et turbida,
> lux intrat, albescit polus,
> Christus uenit, discedite!
>
> A Morning Hymn
> Ye shades of night and turbid clouds,
> Confusion of the world, depart,
> For Light pervades the whitening sky,
> And Christ, the Sun of Justice, comes.

Prudentius (348–ca. 405) is regarded as the greatest poet of the early Latin Church. After leading an active and highly successful political life, he converted to the Roman Catholic faith and retired to a monastery where he devoted himself to poetic composition on religious subjects. His *Cathemerinon* is a book of hymns in praise of God. Considering the opening line of Auden's poem, it is interesting to note that the first hymn of *Liber Cathemerinon* is "Hymnus ad Galli Cantum" ("A Hymn for Cock-Crow").

2   (Opposite line 12 of "The crowing of the cock," p [41].) Edmund Spenser *The Faerie Queene* Canto I (London: William Ponsonbie 1590) 5:

> Enforst to seeke some covert nigh at hand,
>   A shadie grove not farr away they spide,
>   That promist ayde the tempest to
>   withstand:
>   Whose loftie trees yclad with sommers
>   pride,
>   Did spred so broad, that heavens light did
>   hide,
>   Not perceable with power of any starr:
>   And all within were pathes and alleies
>   wide,
>   With footing worne, and leading inward
>   farr:
> Faire harbour that them seemes, so in they
>   entred ar.

"The crowing of the cock"—*P28*, VIII; *P30*, IX; *EA*, 23.

"2" is probably a notation of a possible sequence of poems in an early Auden book (see fn. 2, p [7a] and the opening note to p [33])—or that this is the second version of a poem on one of the excised pages.

1 (Opposite line 31 of "The crowing of the cock," p [43].) Thomas Mann *Der Tod in Venedig* (Berlin: S. Fischer Verlag 1913) 145; Kenneth Burke, tr *Death in Venice* (New York: Alfred A. Knopf 1925) 124:

> Ihm war aber, als ob der bleiche und lieb-liche Psychagog dort draußen ihm lächle, ihm winke; als ob er, die Hand aus der Hüfte lösend, hinausdeute, voranschwebe ins Verheißungsvoll-Ungeheure. Und, wie so oft, machte er sich auf, ihm zu folgen

> (But it seemed to him as though the pale and lovely lure out there were smiling to him; as though, removing his hand from his hip, he were signalling to come out, were guiding towards egregious promises. And, as often before, he stood up to follow him).

The *OED* defines Psychagogue as 'One who directs the mind', derived from the Greek word meaning 'leader of departed souls, said of Hermes'. According to Terence James Reed in the notes to his edition of *Der Tod in Venedig* (Literatur-Kommentare, 19 [Munich: Carl Hanser Verlag 1983] 145–46), the figure of Hermes, as guide of souls to the underworld, came to Mann's attention while he was making notes on the German translation of Plutarch's *Erōtikos*.

2 (Opposite line 42 of "The crowing of the cock," p [43].) Xenophon *Anabasis* IV: vii, 21–24 (The Loeb Classical Library [Cambridge, Mass.: Harvard University Press 1968] 330); Rex Warner, tr *The Persian Expedition* Penguin Classics, 17 (Harmondsworth: Penguin 1952) 165–66:

καὶ ἀφικνοῦνται ἐπὶ τὸ ὄρος τῇ πέμπτῃ ἡμέρᾳˑ ὄνομα δὲ τῷ ὄρει ἦν Θήχης. ἐπεὶ δὲ οἱ πρῶτοι ἐγένοντο ἐπὶ τοῦ ὄρους, κραυγὴ πολλὴ ἐγένετο. ἀκούσας δὲ ὁ Ξενοφῶν καὶ οἱ ὀπισθοφύλακες ᾠήθησαν ἔμπροσθεν ἄλλους ἐπιτίθεσθαι πολεμίουςˑ εἵποντο γὰρ ὄπισθεν ἐκ τῆς καιομένης χώρας, καὶ αὐτῶν οἱ ὀπισθοφύλακες ἀπέκτεινάν τέ τινας καὶ ἐζώγρησαν ἐνέδραν ποιησάμενοι, καὶ γέρρα ἔλαβον δασειῶν βοῶν ὠμοβόεια ἀμφὶ τὰ εἴκοσιν. ἐπειδὴ δὲ βοὴ πλείων τε ἐγίγνετο καὶ ἐγγύτερον καὶ οἱ ἀεὶ ἐπιόντες ἔθεον δρόμῳ ἐπὶ τοὺς ἀεὶ βοῶντας καὶ πολλῷ μείζων ἐγίγνετο ἡ βοὴ ὅσῳ δὴ πλείους ἐγίγνοντο, ἐδόκει δὴ μεῖζόν τι εἶναι τῷ Ξενοφῶντι, καὶ ἀναβὰς ἐφ' ἵππον καὶ Λύκιον καὶ τοὺς ἱππέας ἀναλαβὼν παρεβοήθειˑ καὶ τάχα δὴ ἀκούουσι βοώντων τῶν στρατιωτῶν Θάλαττα θάλαττα καὶ παρεγγυώντων

(They came to the mountains on the fifth day, the name of the mountains being Thekes. When the men in the front reached the summit and caught sight of the sea there was great shouting. Xenophon and the rearguard heard it and thought that there were some more enemies attacking the front, since there were natives of the country they had ravaged following them up behind, and the rearguard had killed some of them and made prisoners of others in an ambush, and captured about twenty raw ox-hide shields, with the hair on. However, when the shouting got louder and drew nearer, and those who were constantly going forward started running towards the men in front who kept shouting, and the more there were of them the more shouting there was, it looked then as though this was something of considerable importance. So Xenophon mounted his horse and, taking Lycus and the cavalry with him, rode forward to give support, and, quite soon, they heard the soldiers shouting out "The Sea! The Sea!" and passing the word down the column).

Xenophon (ca. 430–ca. 354 BC), Greek historian and soldier. Xenophon's *Anabasis* recounts the retreat from the gates of Babylon of a ten-thousand-man Greek expeditionary force which Cyrus the Younger had led against his brother Artaxerxes II, king of Persia. Xenophon led the five-month retreat through rugged terrain, peopled by hostile and warlike tribes. The sight of the Euxine Sea meant that the Greeks, despite the long journey ahead of them, were within striking distance of their home.

3 (Opposite line 45 of "The crowing of the cock," p [43].) [St] John 20:19 (King James Version of the Bible):

> Then the same day at evening, being the first *day* of the week, when the doors were shut where the disciples were assembled for fear of the Jews, came Jesus and stood in the midst, and saith unto them, Peace *be* unto you.

[PAGE 44]

1 (Opposite lines 1–3 of "Nor was that final, for about that time," p [45].) "The Wanderer," lines 45–48 (*The Earliest English Poems: A Bilingual Edition* tr and intro Michael Alexander [Los Angeles: University of California Press 1970] 92–93; hereafter cited as Alexander):

> Ðonne onwæcneð eft   wineleas guma,
> gesihð him biforan   fealwe wegas,
> baþian brimfuglas,   brædan feþra,
> hreosan hrim ond snaw,   hagle gemenged
>
> (Awakeneth after this friendless man,
> seeth before him fallow waves,
> seabirds bathing, broading out feathers,
> snow and hail swirl, hoar-frost falling).

Auden most likely had read the poems in the edition cited by Robert Horace Boyer in his dissertation (University of Pennsylvania 1969), *Anglo-Saxon and Middle English Influences in the Poetry of W. H. Auden*, as that used by Oxford students of the time: Henry Sweet *An Anglo-Saxon Reader in Prose and Verse* (Oxford: Clarendon Press 1904).

2 (Opposite line 4 of "Nor was that final, for about that time," p [45].) "The Dream of the Rood," lines 13–14 (Alexander, 150–51):

> Syllic wæs se sigebeam,   and ic synnum
>   fah,
> forwunded mid wommum
>
> (Stained and marred,
> stricken with shame, I saw the glory-tree).

3 (Opposite line 9 of "Nor was that final, for about that time," p [45].) William Shakespeare *The Tragedy of Antony and Cleopatra* Act IV: scene xiii, 59–68 (*The Complete Works* [Oxford: Clarendon Press 190–] 1165):

> *Cleo:*   Noblest of men, woo't die?
> Hast thou no care of me? shall I abide
> In this dull world, which in thy absence is
> No better than a sty? O, see my women,
>   [*Antony dies.*
> The crown o' the earth doth melt. My lord!
> O, wither'd is the garland of the war,
> The soldier's pole is fall'n; young boys
>   and girls
> Are level now with men; the odds is gone,
> And there is nothing left remarkable
> Beneath the visiting moon.

4 (Opposite line 10 of "Nor was that final, for about that time," p [45].) Ezekiel 37:3:

> And he said unto me, Son of man, can these
>   bones live?
> And I answered, O Lord God, thou
>   knowest.

This vision is a prediction of the restoration of Israel under the figure of the resurrection of the dry bones.

[PAGE 45]

"Nor was that final, for about that time" — *P28*, VII; *P30*, XXIII; *EA*, 24.

Line 11 — saxophone: saxaphone, MS.

[PAGE 46]

"Deemed this an outpost, I" — a version of this poem was published in *Oxford Poetry* 1 (Spring 1984) 90 as the first 24 lines of a longer poem dated ca. October 1927. The poem on this page may have continued onto one of the excised pages.

[PAGE 46, continued]

1   The first stanza of this poem is similar to Po's lyric on p [145].

[PAGE 51]

"Because sap fell away"—*P28*, IX; *EA*, 441.

1   Gabriel Carritt. Auden met Carritt, a Christ Church freshman, in the autumn of 1927.

2   Spears (69) notes that lines 9 and 10 were used in the 1930 poem "Between attention and attention" (*CP*, 22–23: "Make Up Your Mind"):

> Falling in slush,
> Before a friend's friends
> Or shaking hands
> With a snub-nosed winner.

3   Cf John Dryden's "Religio Laici" (*The Poetical Works of Dryden* [Boston: Houghton Mifflin 1950] 167):

> The fly-blown text creates a crawling brood,
> And turns to maggots what was meant for food.

4   "[Lines 13–15 were] turned into prose and used in *The Orators*: 'Love, that notable forked one, riding away from the farm, the ill word said, fought at the frozen dam, transforms itself to influenza and guilty rashes [*EA*, 68–69]'" (Spears, 69).

5   "The 'indolent ulcer' was used in *The Age of Anxiety* [London: Faber 1948 39]" (Spears, 69):

> the Goddess herself
> Presided smiling; a saucy wind,
> Plucking from her thigh her pink wrapper
> Of crêpe-de-chine, disclosed a very
> Indolent ulcer.

It also had been used in line 7 of a poem, dated August 1927, "We, knowing the family history," which was printed in *Oxford Poetry* 1 (Spring 1984) 89–90.

[PAGE 52]

1   (Opposite line 14 of "This the address of the lost soul," p [53].) "The Battle of Maldon," lines 5–8 (Alexander, 162–63):

> þa þæt Offan mæg   ærest onfunde,
> þæt se eorl nolde   yrhðo geþolian,
> he let him þa of handon   leofne fleogan
> hafoc wið þæs holtes,   and to þære hilde stop
>
> (Whereat one of Offa's kin, knowing the Earl
> would not suffer slack-heartedness,
> loosed from his wrist his loved hawk
> over the wood it stooped: he stepped to battle).

Perhaps one should mention that the warrior Wistan appears later in this poem.

[PAGE 53, REV. ON P 54]

"This the address of the lost soul"—*P28*, X ("The mind to body spoke the whole night through"); *EA*, 44. A version of the revision of this poem on p [54] before its final revision there appears in *Oxford Poetry* 1 (Spring 1984) 91–92, "This is the address of the lost soul," dated November 1927.

It seems probable that Auden is making an ironic contrast between the heroic assertion of identity in Browning's "'Childe Roland to the Dark Tower Came'" and the disunity—"A sour union"—of soul and body in this poem.

Line 1—address: adress, MS.

Line 4—preferred: prefered, MS.

Line 13—wood: wood, MS (most likely an intended deletion).

[PAGE 54, REV. OF P 53]

A revised version of this revision appears in *P28*.

1   Cf lines 11–12 of "Truly our fathers had the gout," published in *Oxford Poetry* 1 (Spring 1984) 89, dated August 1927.

Line [1]—address: adress, MS.

Line [3]: light: light, MS (Auden may have intended to cross out this word in his first revision).

Line [4]—preferred: prefered, MS.

[PAGE 57]

"From the very first coming down"—*P28*, XI; *P30*, V; *P34*, 13; *CP*, 44: "The Love Letter"; *CSP*, 60; *SP2*, 9: "The Letter"; *CSP2*, 19; *EA*, 25; *SP4*, 2; *CP2*, 23.

1 The last two lines revise the final lines of a poem, dated August 1927, "We, knowing the family history," published in *Oxford Poetry* 1 (Spring 1984) 89–90.

Line 21—received: recieved, MS.

Line 22—deceived: decieved, MS.

[PAGE 58, REV. OF P 59]

"The four sat on in the bare room"—*P28*, XII; *EA*, 412.

This poem was incorporated into an early version of *Paid on Both Sides* (*EA*, 412). The pencil revisions on line 3 are included in this early version of *Paid on Both Sides*, which was typed in Summer 1928 (those in stanza 3 are in both *P28* and the early version of *Paid on Both Sides*).

1 "'Between attention and attention' . . . takes a line from [this poem]" (Spears, 69):

> The uncertain flesh
> Scraping back chair
> For the wrong train. . . .

2 Cf p [66]: "But he is defeated; let the son," line 9.

Line 3 rev.—duets': duets, MS.

[PAGE 60]

"The colonel to be shot at dawn"—published in *Oxford Poetry* 1 (Spring 1984) 93.

1 Cf "Family Ghosts," line 4 (*CP*, 132).

[PAGE 65]

"To-night, when a full storm surrounds the house"—*P28*, XIII; *P30*, 30: *Paid on Both Sides*; *P34*, 81; *SP*, 33; *SoP*, 16; *CP*, 144: "Remember"; *CSP*, 219; *CLP*, 30; *EA*, 15, 414; *CP2*, 16.

This poem appears in print in two versions. The earlier version—"To-night when a full storm surrounds the house"—is in *P28*; later it was incorporated into *Paid on Both Sides*—"To-night the many come to mind." Katherine Bucknell brought to my attention the resemblance between the early version of this poem and Yeats's elegy "In Memory of Major Robert Gregory" (W. B. Yeats *The Poems* ed Richard J. Finneran [New York: Macmillan 1983] 132).

[PAGE 66, REV. OF P 67]

"But he is defeated; let the son"—*P30*, 34: *Paid on Both Sides*; *P34*, 85; *SP*, 38; *SoP*, 18; *CSP*, 222; *CLP*, 34; *EA*, 17, 416; *CP2*, 19.

1 Cf p [58]: "The four sat on in the bare room," line [12].

[PAGE 67]

1 Cf p [90]: "The Spring will come," line 7.

[PAGE 68, REV. OF P 69b]

"Control of the passes was, he saw, the key"—*P28*, XV; *P30*, XV; *P34*, 26; *CP*, 29: "The Secret Agent"; *CSP*, 44; *CSP2*, 22; *SP3*, 7; *EA*, 25; *SP4*, 3; *CP2*, 25.

As Spears (26) has pointed out, the poem is an unrhymed sonnet.

1 In a letter to John Pudney, July 28 1932 (Berg Collection), Auden wrote: "Re. . . . groups and sex, the two complement each other like day and night. I think there are two great desires which we are always confusing, the desire to be one of a group, building the dam or facing the charging tiger."

2 "[This] line is taken from the Old English poem 'Wulf and Eadwacer', which is the monologue of a captive woman addressed to her outlawed lover (she is on one island, he on another). The line is: 'þæt mon eaþe tosliteð þætte næfre gesomnad wæs' ('They can easily part that which was never joined together', *Exeter Book*, p. 180)" (Fuller, 34).

[PAGE 69: a, b]

The first and second versions of the poem revised on p [68].

[PAGE 89]

"Taller to-day, we remember similar evenings"—*P28*, XVI; *P30*, XXVI; *P34*, 48; *CP*, 113: "As Well as Can Be Expected"; *CSP*, 122: "Taller To-day"; *SP2*, 10; *CSP2*, 20; *EA*, 26; *SP4*, 3; *CP2*, 23.

The second and third stanzas were dropped from the poem in *SP2*.

1 "Captain Ferguson . . . was a sadistic master at [Gabriel Carritt's school, Sedbergh]" (Mendelson, 119).

[PAGE 89, continued]

2 In his dissertation (237), Boyer notes the combination of night and winter images in these two lines and relates them to the following lines from "The Wanderer," lines 101–05 (Alexander, 96–97):

> ond þas stanhleoþu   stormas cnyssað
> hrið hreosende   hrusan bindeð,
> wintres woma,   þonne won cymeð,
> nipeð nihtscua,   norþan onsendeð
> hreo hæglfare   hæleþum on andan

> (Storms break on the stone hillside,
> the ground bound by driving sleet,
> winter's wrath. Then wanness cometh,
> night's shade spreadeth, sendeth from
>   north
> the rough hail to harry mankind).

[PAGE 90]

"The Spring will come"—*P28*, XVII; *P30*, 30: *Paid on Both Sides*; *P34*, 82; *SP*, 34; *SoP*, 17; *CSP*, 219; *CLP*, 31; *EA*, 15, 414; *CP2*, 17. Some of the lines (12–16) had been used in a poem, "Narcissus," dated ca. July 1927, which was published in *Oxford Poetry* I (Spring 1984) 87–89 (see lines 18–20, 26–27).

1 Cf p [67]: "But he is defeated; let the son," line [8].

2 "[These lines] echo . . . the 'Hwær cwom' passage in "The Wanderer," [lines 92–93: Alexander, 94–95]" (Fuller, 28):

> "Hwær cwom mearg? Hwær cwom
>   mago? Hwær cwom maþþumgyfa?
> Hwær cwom symbla gesetu?   Hwær
>   sindon seledreamas? . . ."

> ('Where is that horse now? Where are
>   those men? Where is the hoard-sharer?
> Where is the house of the feast? Where is
>   the hall's uproar? . . .').

Nicholas Jenkins points out in *Oxford Poetry* I (Spring 1984) 87 that the Ten was a cross-country race at Gabriel Carritt's old school, Sedbergh.

Line 16—deceived: decieved, MS.

See also note to p [91: stub], below.

[PAGE 91: STUB]

The following phrase is visible: Not hesitate. This is probably a marginal revision to an earlier version of the poem on p [90] (see line 2).

[PAGE 93]

"The summer quickens grass"—*P28*, XVIII; *P30*, 29: *Paid on Both Sides* ("The summer quickens all"); *P34*, 80; *SP*, 32; *SoP*, 15; *CP*, 230 (Songs XXXIII); *CSP*, 218; *CLP*, 30; *EA*, 14, 413; *CP2*, 16.

After one discarded revision of the original first stanza, Auden condensed the first two stanzas at the right of the second stanza. In *Paid on Both Sides* this poem takes the form of a dialogue between Anne and John.

Line 4 rev.—compel: compell, MS.

[PAGE 95]

"'Grow thin by walking, and go inland'"—a version of this poem, probably a revision of this but also dated April 1928, was published in *Oxford Poetry* I (Spring 1984) 93–94.

1 Cf p [103]: "To throw away the key and walk away," line 3.

2 Cf p [169]: "Under boughs between our tentative endearments," line 6.

3 See p [103]: "To throw away the key and walk away," line [24].

4 Cf p [103]: "To throw away the key and walk away," line [30].

[PAGE 96]

"Some say that handsome raider still at large"—*P28*, XIX; *P30*, 28: *Paid on Both Sides*; *P34*, 80; *SP*, 32; *SoP*, 15; *CSP*, 218; *CLP*, 29; *EA*, 14; *CP2*, 15.

See also note to p [99: stub], below.

[PAGE 99: STUB]

The following phrase is visible: At on. This is probably a marginal revision to an earlier version of the poem on p [96] (see line 8).

[PAGE 101]

"Often the man, alone shut, shall consider"—
P30, 14: *Paid on Both Sides*; *P34*, 65; *SP*, 16; *SoP*,
11; *CSP*, 205; *CLP*, 17; *EA*, 5, 411; *CP2*, 7.

1   Fuller (18) suggests a comparison of these
opening lines with those of "The Wanderer,"
lines 1–17 (Alexander, 90–91):

> Oft him anhaga   are gebideð,
> metudes miltse,   þeah þe he modcearig
> geond lagulade   longe sceolde
> hreran mid hondum   hrimcealde sæ,
> wadan wræclastas.   Wyrd bið ful aræd!
> Swa cwæð eardstapa,   earfeþa gemyndig,
> wraþra wælsleahta,   winemæga hryre

> (Who liveth alone longeth for mercy,
> Maker's mercy. Though he must traverse
> tracts of sea, sick at heart,
> —trouble with oars ice-cold waters,
> the ways of exile—Wierd is set fast.
> Thus spoke such a 'grasshopper', old griefs
>   in mind,
> cold slaughters, the death of dear kinsmen).

2   Boyer (202) notes the similarity between the
lines "Spring came, urging to ships, a casting-
off, / But one would stay, vengeance not done"
and the following lines from *Beowulf* (Benjamin
Thorpe, tr [New York: Barron's Educational
Series 1962] 76):

> Ðâ wæs winter scacen,   fæger foldan
>   bearm,
> fundode wrecca,   gist of geardum;
> he tô gyrn-wræce   swiðor þôhte
> þonne tô sæ-lâde

> (Then was winter departed, earth's bosom
>   fair,
> the stranger hasten'd, the guest from
>   the dwellings:
> he on wily vengeance was more intent
> than on a sea-voyage).

[PAGES 103 AND 105]

"To throw away the key and walk away"—*P28*,
XX; *P30*, 25: *Paid on Both Sides*; *P34*, 76; *SP*, 28;
CP, 145: "The Walking Tour"; *CSP*, 215; *SP2*,
11: "The Journey"; *CLP*, 27; *EA*, 12; *CP2*, 14.
    "Technically [this poem] marks Auden's first
use of the slant-rhymes with initial consonance

(right/rate, wall/well) that he found in Wilfred
Owen's 'Strange Meeting' and used frequently
in the next two years" (Mendelson, 54).

1   Fuller (262) compares this line with "But left
and right alternately / Is consonant with History"
in *New Year Letter* (London: Faber 1941) 155.
Also, cf p [95]: "'Grow thin by walking, and go
inland,'" line 8.

2   Cf Yeats's "Byzantium" (*The Poems*, 248),
lines 9–12:

> Before me floats an image, man or shade,
> Shade more than man, more image than a
>   shade;
> For Hades' bobbin bound in mummy-cloth
> May unwind the winding path. . . .

3   "Auden dropped the lines about the bone's
bane within a few weeks of writing them, but it
is evident that he did this not to alter the poem's
vision of defeat but to clarify its structure" (Men-
delson, 55).

4   Cf p [142]: "Always the following wind of
history," line 19.

5   See p [95]: "'Grow thin by walking, and go
inland,'" line 15.

6   "'Not swooping at the surface still like gulls
/ But with prolonged drowning shall develop
gills.' (Probably an allusion is intended here to
the 'destructive element' passage in Conrad's
Lord Jim [London: William Blackwood 1900,
228])" (Spears, 17).

> "A man that is born falls into a dream like a
> man who falls into the sea. If he tries to
> climb out into the air as inexperienced
> people endeavour to do, he drowns—nicht
> war? . . . No! I tell you! The way is to the
> destructive element submit yourself, and
> with the exertions of your hands and feet
> in the water make the deep, deep sea keep
> you up."

7   Cf p [95]: "'Grow thin by walking, and go
inland,'" line 19.

8   "In August 1928, not long after leaving
Oxford, [Auden] spent three weeks in Spa in

[PAGES 103 AND 105, note 8, continued]

Belgium—'staying with a psychologist,' he said in a letter. Exactly what happened there is unknown. Almost certainly he took some sort of treatment, and there are indications that he did this in the hope of altering his sexual preferences. Little could have been accomplished in so short a period, and little was. Auden seems to have regarded the whole episode, then and afterward, with amused disdain. The poems he wrote on his return to England showed no change in his conviction that his isolation was congenital and incurable" (Mendelson, 54).

Line 27—alleging: alledging, MS.

Line 31—Receive: Recieve, MS.

[PAGE 117]

"The Spring unsettles sleeping partnerships"—*P30*, 17: *Paid on Both Sides*; *P34*, 69; *SP*, 20; *SoP*, 14; *CP*, 131: "It's Too Much"; *CSP*, 208; *CLP*, 20; *EA*, 7; *CP2*, 9.

Line 11—mortgaged: morgaged, MS.

[PAGE 119: a, b]

"No, not from this life, not from this life is any" / "Who's jealous of his latest company"—*P30*, 8: *Paid on Both Sides* ("Not from this life, not from this life is any"); *P34*, 60; *SP*, 10; *SoP*, 9; *CP*, 83: "All Over Again"; *CSP*, 200; *CLP*, 12; *EA*, 2; *CP2*, 4.

1   Cf p [173]: "Love by ambition," line 12.

2   "On his return from Spa [Auden] visited the McElwees in Somerset; but *Paid on Both Sides* was not performed during his visit as he had intended it to be. 'They refused to do the play,' he wrote to Isherwood, 'as they say the village won't stand it'" (Carpenter, 82).

Version a, line 5—Who's: Whose, MS.

Version a, line [9]—Receive: Recieve, MS.

[PAGE 123]

"Can speak of trouble, pressure on men"—*P30*, 8: *Paid on Both Sides*; *P34*, 60; *SP*, 11; *SoP*, 9; *CP*, 24: "Always in Trouble"; *CSP*, 201; *CLP*, 13; *EA*, 2; *CP2*, 4.

[PAGE 124]

"There is the city"—*P30*, 24: *Paid on Both Sides*; *P34*, 75; *SP*, 27; *CSP*, 214; *CLP*, 26; *EA*, 11; *CP2*, 13.

"Auden had never written in a tone anything like this before. He allows no irony, no threats, no ambiguous silence to intrude on his visions of triumph.

"In Auden's notebook this poem appears as an independent work, and there is no way of knowing whether, at the time he wrote it, he planned to use it as one of John Nower's speeches in a revised *Paid on Both Sides*—a context in which the poem's promise is qualified by Nower's defeat. (Verses undoubtedly written for the revised version of the charade appear in Auden's notebook in the following month.) Whatever Auden's plans for it, the poem marks his discovery of a rhetoric for hope and metaphors for freedom. Now he could write about a future that had hitherto been closed to his poetry" (Mendelson, 58).

Line 22—leat: 'An open watercourse to conduct water for . . . mills, mining works etc.', *OED*.

[PAGE 135: STUB]

The following letter is visible: E? It is probably the marginal revision to the first line of a poem excised from this page.

[PAGE 141]

"If I lived in the country and you lived in the town"—*P30*, 23: *Paid on Both Sides* ("Sametime sharers of the same house"); *P34*, 74; *SP*, 26; *CSP*, 213; *CLP*, 25; *EA*, 11; *CP*, 12.

Most of this poem was used as part of the dialogue between John Nower and the Spy.

Line 7—sametime: Auden did not intend to write "sometime" (a misreading in later versions).

[PAGE 142]

"Always the following wind of history"—*P30*, 16: *Paid on Both Sides*; *P34*, 68; *SP*, 19; *SoP*, 13; *CSP*, 207; *CLP*, 19; *EA*, 7; *CP2*, 8.

1   Cf p [103]: "To throw away the key and walk away," line [12].

[PAGE 143]

"Because I'm come, it does not mean to hold"—*P30*, 20: *Paid on Both Sides*; *P34*, 71; *SP*, 23; *CSP*, 210; *CLP*, 22; *EA*, 9; *CP2*, 10.

"The half-rhymed couplets of [this poem] are remarkably similar in tone not only to those of the choruses—'The Spring unsettles sleeping partnerships' and 'To throw away the key and walk away'—but also to those of the early poem 'Venus Will Now Say a Few Words' (*CSP*, 33). The similarity is striking enough to suggest a common origin, perhaps a planned longer poem" (Fuller, 24).

1   Mendelson (51) quotes from Auden's 1929 journal:

> Among the educated classes the child very soon connects [?by] suggestion the idea of physical contact and sexual acts. When he does gratify the first, he thinks he wants the second, i.e. when he sleeps with his friend he gets an erection. "Mother told us that's what flowers did" [the child explains to the friend].

2   "Soon after writing *Paid on Both Sides*, [Auden] told Stephen Spender, 'I am the Man-Woman.' Presumably he was alluding not only to his homosexuality but also to the role he imagined for himself as an agent of healing impulse and as an isolated noncommunicative poetic voice which must warn, as the Man-Woman does in the charade, that 'where I am / All talking is forbidden'" (Mendelson, 51).

[PAGE 144]

"Yesterday we sat at table together"—*P30*, 24: *Paid on Both Sides*; *P34*, 75; *SP*, 27; *CSP*, 214; *CLP*, 25; *EA*, 11; *CP2*, 13.

In *Paid on Both Sides* part of this poem appears as a dialogue between Dick and John.

[PAGE 145: a, b]

"In these days during the migration, days" and "Past victory is honour, to accept"—*P30*, 19: *Paid on Both Sides*; *P34*, 70; *SP*, 21; *CSP*, 209; *CLP*, 21; *EA*, 8; *CP2*, 10.

Bo and Po are characters in *Paid on Both Sides*.

[PAGES 151 AND 153]

"We made all possible preparations"—*P30*, XII; *P34*, 23; *CP*, 156: "Let History Be My Judge"; *CSP*, 165; *CSP2*, 24; *EA*, 26; *CP2*, 27.

[PAGE 155]

"Again in conversations"—*P30*, VIII; *P34*, 17; *CP*, 5: "Two's Company"; *CSP*, 21: "Never Stronger"; *CSP2*, 25; *EA*, 27; *CP2*, 28.

[PAGE 157]

"Head asleep"—unpublished.

1   Cf "The Wanderer," line 14 (*CP*, 34).

Line 21—Receive: Recieve, MS.

[PAGE 158: a–g]

Shorts—Of the seven "Shorts" on this page, only f was published (slightly revised): "The friends of the born nurse / Are always getting worse" (*CSP2*, 42; *EA*, 51; *CP2*, 41).

Short c, line 1—bachelor: batchelor, MS.

[PAGES 163 AND 165]

"From scars where kestrels hover"—*P30*, XXIV; *P34*, 44; *CP*, 43: "Missing"; *CSP*, 58; *CSP2*, 20; *EA*, 28; *CP2*, 24. A similar poem, dated ca. December 1927, with many of the same lines, "The weeks of blizzard over," appears in *Oxford Poetry* 1 (Spring 1984) 92–93.

1   Boyer (249) notes a similar use of sea birds as part of a tone of isolation and uneasiness in "The Seafarer," lines 17–26 (Alexander, 98–99):

> haegl scurum fleag.
> þær ic ne gehyrde   butan hlimman sæ,
> iscaldne wæg.   Hwilum ylfete song
> dyde ic me to gomene,   ganetes hleoþor
> ond huilpan sweg   fore hleahtor wera,
> mæw singende   fore medodrince.
> Stormas þær stanclifu beotan,   þær him
>   stearn oncwæð
> isigfeþera;   ful oft þæt earn bigeal,
> urigfeþra;   ne ænig hleomæga
> feasceaftig ferð   frefran meahte
> (Hail flew in showers,
> there was no sound there but the slam
>   of waves
> along an icy sea. The swan's blare

[PAGES 163 AND 165, note 1, continued]

> my seldom amusement; for men's laughter
> there was curlew-call, there were the cries
> of gannets,
> for mead-drinking the music of the gull.
> To the storm striking the stone cliffs
> gull would answer, eagle scream
> from throats frost-feathered. No friend
> or brother
> by to speak the despairing mind).

2   " 'The slow fastidious line / That disciplines the fell', would seem to have an even earlier origin in a poem dating from Auden's schooldays which describes 'the long slow curvings of the fells' on Alston Moor" (Fuller, 263). See E. R. Dodds in *Shenandoah* XVIII (Winter 1967) 9: "His earliest poem, as he has told us himself, was 'a Wordsworthian sonnet on Blea Tarn in the Lake District.' In another unpublished piece he admires 'the long slow curvings of the fells' on Alston Moor, and finds 'their coldness tenderest warmth, their dumbness words.' "

3   "Lines 6–14, and the final line and a half ["and pass / Alive into the house"] are taken from *Poems* (1928), No. II ["I chose this lean country," lines 5–13 (with a change of tense) and the final line and a half]" (Fuller, 33).

4   In *Lions and Shadows* (London: The Hogarth Press 1938) 265–70, Christopher Isherwood describes a drunken journey taken by himself and a friend:

> We drove on, across the misty bog-plains, striped black where peat had been cut, in the direction of Cape Wrath. The coast was gashed into jagged fjords: under the cliffs, the water lay like ebony, with vivid jade shallows.

Cape Wrath is a promontory in the extreme NW of Scotland, ten miles WNW of Durness. As Fuller (32) has pointed out, the reference is meant to be ironic.

Line 9—unforeseen: unforsen, MS.

Line 34—capital: capitle, MS.

[PAGES 169 AND 171]

"Under boughs between our tentative endearments, how should we hear"—*P30*, XXVIII;

P34, 51; *CP*, 147: "When the Devil Drives"; *CSP*, 156; *EA*, 29.

The pencilled "1" on this poem and the "2" on "The crowing of the cock" p [41] are probably a tentative numbering for a sequence of poems that became *P30*.

1   Cf p [95]: " 'Grow thin by walking, and go inland,' " line 12.

[PAGE 172]

"Put your legs on the table"—unpublished.

[PAGES 173 AND 175]

"Love by ambition"— *P30*, X; *P34*, 20; *CP*, 78: "Too Dear, Too Vague"; *CSP*, 94; *CSP2*, 28; *EA*, 30; *CP2*, 30.

1   Cf p [119a]: "No, not from this life, not from this life is any," line [10].

2   "The second part of the poem carries echoes of Lawrence's arguments about 'sex in the head', and Auden may have in mind, in his lines about leaving 'the North in place / With a good grace', Lawrence's elaboration of his theory about the four poles of the dynamic psyche (see *Fantasia of the Unconscious*, Heinemann, 1961, pp. 100ff.)" (Fuller, 38).

Line 23—aggression: agression, MS.

[PAGE 181]

"Before this loved one"—*P30*, XVIII; *P34*, 34; *CP*, 19: "This One"; *CSP*, 36; *SP2*, 16; *CSP2*, 26: "This Loved One"; *EA*, 31; *CP2*, 28.

This seems to be a hastily written fair copy of a version of the poem on an excised page—the odd punctuation in lines 17–19 was removed by *P30*.

1   Spears (70) quotes Louis MacNeice on Auden's use of the word "ghost" (from *Modern Poetry* [Oxford: Oxford University Press 1938] 172):

> Auden's view of the world encourag[ed] him to use certain words in specialized senses. For example, he sometimes seems to use the word 'ghost' to denote either hereditary influence or a man's own slant backwards towards his parents or ancestors. Auden [was] much occupied with the paradoxes of family relationships.

2   Fuller (37) notes the influence of Laura Rid-
ing in this poem, and compares lines 24–29:

> And smiling of
> This gracious greeting
> 'Good day, good luck'
> Is no real meeting
> But instinctive look
> A backward love.
>   (*EA*, 31)

with parts of two Riding poems—"All Nothing,
Nothing" and "Rhythms of Love" (*The Poems of
Laura Riding* [New York: Persea Books 1980] 103
and 114):

> The standing-stillness,
> The from foot-to-foot,
> Is no real illness,
> Is no real fever.
>
> *   *   *   *
>
> We shall say: Love is no more
> Than waking, smiling,
> Forcing out 'good morning'.

Line 23—mortgaged: morgaged, MS.

[PAGE 183]

"Watch any day his nonchalant pauses; see"—
P30, IV; *P34*, 12; *SP*, 45; *SoP*, 21; *CP*, 152: "We
All Make Mistakes"; *CSP*, 160: "A Free One";
CSP2, 29; *EA*, 31; *SP4*, 4; *CP2*, 31.

1   "(Compare 'iron wood' with Pope's 'iron
harvests' in his *Essay on Man*, IV, l. 12)" (Fuller,
38). Pope is asking where Happiness is to be
found: "Twin'd with the wreaths Parnassian
laurels yield, / Or reap'd in iron harvests of the
field?"

[PAGE 188: STUB]

This is a very tentative reading of the remnants
of rapidly written ends of lines of verse (proba-
bly marginal revisions) that may provide a clue
to the poem, possibly in three-line stanzas, that
was excised from this page.

[PAGE 191]

A J A is Alan J. Ansen, Auden's pupil and friend.
The handwriting is Ansen's. As Ansen noted in
the transcription accompanying his gift to the
Berg Collection, on Christmas Eve 1949 Auden
presented Ansen with this notebook. During the
course of the evening they discussed Paul
Cadmus' series of paintings *The Seven Deadly
Sins*, and Auden gave his own list, initially with
Lust in the least serious position.

Index of First Lines and Titles

The poems in the notebook and transcription are listed alphabetically by first lines and by titles used by Auden in later editions of his work. Other poems by Auden mentioned in the notes are indexed. There are also references to Auden's own notes in the notebook. Page references are to the original pagination of the notebook, bracketed at the foot of each transcription page.

Set in Bembo and printed by the Meriden-Stinehour Press, Lunenburg, Vermont,
on Mohawk Superfine Text, an acid-free paper. Facsimile photography by the Meriden-Stinehour Press.
Slipcase and binding by Judi Conant, Guildhall, Vermont.

Design by Marilan Lund

Label by Jerry Kelly